COACHING Cross Country SUCCESSFULLY

Joe Newton
York High School, Elmhurst, Illinois

with Joe Henderson
Runner's World Magazine

Human Kinetics

Library of Congress Cataloging-in-Publication Data

Newton, Joe, 1929-
    Coaching cross country successfully / Joe Newton with Joe
Henderson.
        p.   cm.
    Includes index.
    ISBN 0-88011-701-X
    1. Cross-country running--Coaching.   I. Henderson, Joe, 1943-   .
  II. Title.
  GV1063.2.C63N49   1998
  796.42--dc21

07-35197
CIP

ISBN: 0-88011-701-X

Developmental Editor: Jim Kestner
Managing Editor: Lynn M. Hooper-Davenport
Assistant Editors: Erin Cler, Sandra Merz Bott, and Erin Sprague
Copyeditor: Jim Burns
Proofreader: Erin Cler
Indexer: Theresa Schaefer
Graphic Designer: Nancy Rasmus
Graphic Artist: Francine Hamerski
Photo Editor: Boyd LaFoon
Cover Designer: Jack Davis
Photographer (cover): Tom Roberts
Photographer (interior): Tom Roberts (pages 30, 35, 57, 91)
Illustrators: Joe Bellis and Tom Roberts
Printer: Versa Press

Unless otherwise noted, all interior photos were provided courtesy of the author and York High School, Elmhurst, Illinois.

Copies of this book are available at special discounts for bulk purchase for sales promotions, premiums, fund-raising, or educational use. Special editions or book excerpts can also be created to specification. For details, contact the Special Sales Manager at Human Kinetics.

Printed in the United States of America   10 9 8 7 6 5 4 3

Human Kinetics
Web site: www.humankinetics.com

United States: Human Kinetics
P.O. Box 5076
Champaign, IL 61825-5076
800-747-4457
e-mail: humank@hkusa.com

Canada: Human Kinetics
475 Devonshire Road, Unit 100
Windsor, ON N8Y 2L5
800-465-7301 (in Canada only)
e-mail: orders@hkcanada.com

Europe: Human Kinetics
Units C2/C3 Wira Business Park
West Park Ring Road
Leeds LS16 6EB, United Kingdom
+44 (0)113 278 1708
e-mail: hk@hkeurope.com

Australia: Human Kinetics
57A Price Avenue
Lower Mitcham, South Australia 5062
08 8277 1555
e-mail: liahka@senet.com.au

New Zealand: Human Kinetics
P.O. Box 105-231, Auckland Central
09-523-3462
e-mail: hkp@ihug.co.nz

CONTENTS

Part IV   Coaching for Competitions

Part V   Coaching Evaluation

FOREWORD

Joe Newton has been an unbelievably successful cross country coach. His teams have won an incredible 19 Illinois State High School Championships between the 1960s and the mid-1990s. In 1988, he was the first high school coach ever named to the men's Olympic coaching staff.

Many traits and talents lie behind his success. The first is his unflagging enthusiasm for the sport and for helping young people, even after almost four decades on the job. His other strengths include a great ability to communicate and to motivate. He is an effective recruiter who always has masses of young runners out for his teams, from which he draws an extremely talented top-seven scorers.

Despite his large numbers of athletes, he is able to relate closely to each of them. He makes a point to shake the hand of every runner every day and call each one by name. This close and constant attention creates a fine sense of team camaraderie and cohesion.

No other coach in the United States has a greater impact on the sport of cross country than Joe Newton. Through this book, all coaches can benefit from Joe's ideas about organization, promotion, and recruiting as well as from his knowledge of the technical aspects of training and racing.

Sam Bell
Head Track and Cross Country Coach
Indiana University

ACKNOWLEDGMENTS

To my mother, Blanche, for her love and kindness, and my father, Joseph, for his strength and discipline.

To my wife, Joan, for her love, patience, and support that allowed me to coach in the first place.

To Ed O'Farrell Sr., my high school coach, who took special interest in me and allowed me to be a coach.

To Rut Walter, my coach at Northwestern, who was like a second father to me.

To Arthur Lydiard, who taught me his marathon training system.

To Sam Bell, Indiana University track coach, who has been my friend and mentor all these years.

To Dr. John F. Durkin for his great support in always having the York High School athletes "ready on the day."

To Dr. Joe Vigil, Adams State cross country coach, my friend for more than 20 years who taught me the ins and outs of $\dot{V}O_2$max training.

To Dr. Tom Tutko, the great San Jose State psychologist, who taught me about people and how to handle my athletes.

And finally, to Peter Coe, who taught me how, when, and why to apply speed training, and who shared his son Sebastian with my family.

Joe Newton

AUTHOR NOTES

My first career goal wasn't to be a writer of running books, but to be a coach of runners. The highest calling of an experienced runner, I used to think, is to pass the baton of knowledge to the later generations of runners. The best people to coach, I used to think, are the young who are new to the sport and ready to make quick and dramatic performance leaps with the right guidance. These remain my beliefs today.

I settled for second best and became a writer. Whatever "coaching" I've done is secondhand, by way of the printed page instead of direct instruction-giving, mistake-correcting, and encouragement-shouting. While loving my job, I envy what you coaches get to do. And I admire no other coach more than Joe Newton for all he has done—for all the winning over four decades, of course, but even more so for all the young people he has set on a good course for life. The letters from his ex-athletes, which open each part of this book, attest to his enduring influence.

Coaches who want to do their job better will ask the masters of their profession for advice. As a writer, my job is also to ask questions of experts. So this book takes the form of an extended clinic on paper. You read here the answers to hundreds of questions and concerns about cross country, posed to one of the most successful coaches in history.

A note on pronouns used here. The "I" refers to Joe Newton. The "we" means his program at York High School, and the "you" is his fellow coach who reads this book. Joe Newton coaches only the young men at York. However, the advice applies equally to the coaching of young women, and pronoun references to runners are gender-neutral.

The book is written primarily for coaches, and focuses on high school cross country. But the runners themselves and their parents can profit by reading this material, and much of it translates to the track racing that these athletes are likely to do between cross country seasons. Pass this book around. Freely share it the way Joe Newton shares his knowledge with you.

Joe Henderson

INTRODUCTION

This book took about a half century and an entire coaching career to write, so it had better be good! *Coaching Cross Country Successfully* is for you coaches who up to now have had to learn from trial and error, general coaching manuals, distance running books, or coaching colleagues. This is the first book written specifically for you, the cross country coach, explaining the key principles of coaching our sport.

But exactly what kind of cross country coaching book is it? One that's filled with time-tested workouts? One that covers the basics of teaching distance running techniques? One that recommends a variety of communication and motivational methods to gain from athletes their interest and then their strong desire to excel? One that presents a detailed blueprint for building and implementing a program and plan? Or one that shares true stories of success and failure?

It is all of the above—and more. Now you know why it took me so long to write it! With the help of *Runner's World* writer Joe Henderson, I present in *Coaching Cross Country Successfully* the sound principles of developing a cross country team and individuals who will perform at their best. The five parts of the book—developing a coaching foundation, planning, teaching, coaching meets, and evaluating athletes and your program—are the cornerstones of any successful coaching career.

Nothing against football, basketball, and the other so-called major sports, but how many sports fans in the U.S. know that cross country ranks *fifth* in participation among sports offered at the high school level for boys and girls? And how many know that the sport has several hundred college programs and a growing international presence?

Cross country *is* a major sport that has received far too little attention. You coaches need to do something about that! You need to promote our sport, to generate more enthusiasm for it, and to create greater community awareness of it. In *Coaching Cross Country Successfully*, I'll give you plenty of ideas and examples of how to spread the word and get a great response to your message.

At York High School in Elmhurst, Illinois, we've been fortunate to enjoy the kind of success that many coaches and athletes only dream about. Much more important than the facts and figures of championships won, though, is the intangible contribution cross country makes to our school and community.

We have more than 150 runners try out for our team each season, because they want to be part of something successful. It's not just about winning, you understand. It's about being part of a tradition where discipline, effort, skill, and teamwork are of the utmost importance. Our young runners show a great desire to make the lifestyle changes and sacrifices that many of their peers consider too extreme.

Most important, the athletes take the lessons from their cross country careers and apply them to their schoolwork and jobs to achieve a similar high level of success. That's what really matters in the long run.

I've learned a lot—especially from my athletes—in the last 40-some years. Now I'd like to share what I've learned in hopes that *Coaching Cross Country Successfully* will help you and your athletes enjoy the great experiences the sport has given me. Let's get started.

Joe Newton

Part I

COACHING FOUNDATION

Letter from a former York athlete to Joe Newton:

I can assure you that every fall I think back to 1968 and 1969, and wonder how you and the current crop of athletes are getting along. It certainly makes me smile and feel proud to find that you have won yet another state championship.

Next month I will be 40 years old. If my mental arithmetic is correct, this means I am older than you were when I ran for you. I still think about you a lot and feel the lessons that I learned at York High School under your guidance are valuable to me in my everyday life. I know that the championships are very exciting, but more important to me are the lessons that you taught us about life itself.

Most of what one reads in the media about young people sounds rather negative these days, but I know that this is not the entire spectrum of what is really going on. It is reassuring to me to know that you are still there at York and still contributing to the development of young people.

Mark L. Schmelzel, MD
Class of 1970

Chapter 1

DEVELOPING A COACHING PHILOSOPHY

Cross country is a school-based sport in the United States, with its season lasting only a couple of months each fall. But make no mistake, this is a year-round and even career-long preoccupation for its coaches and athletes. As soon as one cross country season ends, preparation for the next one begins. It begins for coaches by analyzing the season past and planning to make improvements in the one to come. It begins for athletes by training for future seasons (including indoor and outdoor track, where most runners compete in the winter and spring).

For both coaches and athletes one year provides a springboard to the next. By working consistently, they all improve over the long haul. Over a career the coach develops a personal philosophy for guiding the program. The runner at least develops a love for and commitment to running that lasts well beyond the school years and at best carries away lessons for life from working with the coach and teammates.

This opening chapter shows you how one coach's philosophy developed for one team, and how you can create such guidelines of your own—whether you're coaching at a big or small school, with a boys' or girls' team, or with an established or new program.

DEVELOPING AN INTEREST

Don't think you must have experience as a distance runner to coach distance runners. And don't think you must have been an outstanding athlete to succeed as a coach. I never ran any distance races as a young athlete. The only long running I did was as a training device.

My specialties were the sprints and long jump. This was so long ago that athletes still ran 100 and 220 *yards*, and they called my field event the *broad* jump. At Parker High School on the south side of Chicago I was a jack-of-all-trades and a master of none. My best marks were 10-flat in the 100, 22.8 in the 220, and 21-7 in the long jump.

At Northwestern University my marks improved to 9.8, 21.4, and 22-10. I was never a great athlete, but had to work very hard to make it. This work ethic would help me later on as a coach. Because I had to work like the devil for a little bit of success, I have empathy for the little person. I've always helped anyone who was willing to pay the price.

Finding Inspiration

Each one of you probably can point to your own coaches who inspired you to follow in their footsteps. Two of my coaches influenced me in my choice of career and in the way I coach. Number one was Ed O'Farrell Sr., my high school coach in basketball and track. He was a tough, demanding guy, and I just loved him.

Rut Walter, a coach of mine at Northwestern, was the opposite. He was a quiet guy who never seemed to get really excited. His strength was that he paid attention to his athletes and made them feel good about themselves. These two men inspired me to go into coaching. I see my approach as a combination of theirs. I can be tough and demanding, but I also pay close attention to my athletes and try to make them feel good about themselves.

Luck plays a part in your career path, and I've been very lucky. When I graduated from Northwestern, my dad made me go right on and get my master's degree. It was not my plan at the time, but he said, "You're going to need your master's if you want to teach." So I continued in school.

No sooner was my degree in hand than my draft call came. The army sent me to Fort Leonard Wood, Missouri. Someone in personnel saw in my records that I was trained in physical education. While the rest of my unit went to Korea, I went to the fieldhouse as a basketball and track coach from 1952 to '54.

I had two future Olympians on my track team, Phil Coleman and Ted Wheeler. I still competed in the sprints but had a growing fascination with distance runners like Phil and Ted. They impressed me with how hard they worked.

Coming out of the service, my first job was in Waterman, Illinois, a little town with about 1,000 population. About 50 people applied, but I got the job because the principal was also a Northwestern graduate.

Marius Bakken, 1995 West Suburban Conference champion, sprints with 100 meters to go.

Starting Small

Waterman High School only had about 100 students (K-12), and I had to coach all the sports. The school didn't have football but played baseball in the fall. I started a cross country team my second year at the school, which meant I had to run back and forth between one practice and the other.

Darryl Bremner played baseball and ran cross country that fall. He'd practice baseball, then run around the outfield a few times to train for his races. He was the best runner on the team, which a five-minute miler could be back then. We won the conference cross country title that first year, which goes to show that it doesn't take a long time to build a winning program if you work at it.

After my second year at Waterman I read in the *Chicago Daily News* that legendary track coach Charley East had retired at York High School in Elmhurst. An assistant would take over, leaving a position open. I was one of 125 coaches to apply. Another Northwestern

Coach Newton embraces the boys in a moment of pure ecstasy.

graduate was the personnel director, and he picked me. I've only had two jobs in my life, and both came because I went to the right university.

By then I'd fallen in love with cross country but wasn't coaching it, having spent four years as an assistant in football as well as track. Then in quick succession the head track coach moved to a new school and the cross country coach also resigned. Nineteen sixty was a very good year for me. I was promoted to head coach in both sports and have stayed here ever since.

DEVELOPING A PROGRAM

My advice to you coaches is not to feel discouraged if you inherit a lackluster program. York started cross country in 1939 and had never even won a conference championship. The previous three years they had ranked near the bottom. My first look at the York team might have been depressing, but it wasn't. I looked at it as an opportunity, since we could only improve.

One problem was that the runners didn't work hard enough. I remember in previous years when I was going out for our football practices, the cross country team would already be coming *back* from theirs. "What is this?" I thought. "They've only been out there for a half hour."

They only had 8 or 10 guys on the team. There was no enthusiasm. They didn't care if they were any good or not. All they wanted to do was win their letter.

You have to take the raw material you have and build from there. I didn't want to drive anyone away, because we didn't have many runners to spare. My job was to get guys out for the sport and raise the enthusiasm level so we could start improving. We had 15 or 20 my first year, which was double the size of the previous team.

Right from the start I went to every freshman gym class and tried to recruit runners. I wanted the young kids who still had a good attitude toward sports and who would be around for the next four years to develop as athletes.

The training then was still quite modest by today's standards. One day I gave these guys five 220s in about 35 seconds each. They were in agony—cramps and all the rest. This was a major workout for them.

Our goal that first year was to win *one* dual meet and not finish last in the eight-team conference meet. We were 4-3 in duals and finished fifth in the conference. The next year, 1961, our record improved again and we qualified for the state meet, where we placed seventh.

I can remember like it was yesterday sitting in the stands when the awards were presented. The winning team from Highland Park was ecstatic. Its coach, Dick Ault (a former Olympic hurdler and world record-holder) was screaming and hugging his athletes. I thought, "What I'd give to do that someday!" Little did I know that "someday" was only one year away.

Working at Winning

In 1962 a young athlete named Fred Logan became my unofficial assistant coach on the course. He paid the price and inspired the other runners to do the same. Fred was my first runner who trained in the summer, and he got others to join him in these preseason workouts. He was also the first to run in the morning, and he got four or five others to join him then.

That year, my third at York, we won the state cross country title. Fred Logan placed 10th in the state, and he became the prototype of the overachieving York athlete who made up for limited talent with hard work. After that the program took off like a snowball rolling downhill.

DEVELOPING COACHING EXCELLENCE

Stick to these guidelines, and you'll develop excellence in your coaching.

Nancy Klatt of York maintains her lead over the Willow Brook's Shelly McBride, 1986.

1. Make the sport important so the athlete can gain status from it.
2. Adopt a positive approach to everything you do and say.
3. Set realistic goals that challenge but don't overwhelm the athletes.
4. Realize that success is based on overcoming disappointments and bad days.
5. Develop a winning attitude by repeating satisfying experiences.
6. Take a sincere interest in every one of your athletes.

7. Deal with the whole person—mind, body, and spirit.
8. Stress self-improvement for all athletes.
9. Develop thinkers who will make suggestions for their own improvement.
10. Promote group dynamics and the magic of team togetherness.
11. Let the athletes know it is *their* program.
12. Stay in shape yourself so you can be a role model.

DEVELOPING A PHILOSOPHY

As a coach you have to love your job and the kids. If you do, you'll be enthusiastic and you'll work hard. You'll lead by example. You also have to be *you*, developing your own philosophy and standing on it.

As a coach you're always refining your approach. I'm still making changes now, after almost 40 years on the job. The main change I made early was to expect a lot more training from the athletes. For instance, Dick Ault's Highland Park team that won the state title the year before we did was doing a workout of 10 half miles, which had been unheard of for us. We started doing interval halves.

Philosophically, the main change in me over the years is that I now listen better. As a young coach I was great at shouting orders, but I didn't listen to the runners' legitimate complaints. I was a disciplinarian who did some things that were pretty harsh.

You must have rules, and you still must be the boss. Kids need guidelines and really want discipline. But you also must be careful not to be overbearing, and you must never, ever demean them. In addition, you have to be careful not to pound the athletes to death and drive them away from the sport.

The men of Group Six show their spirit by wearing ties to practice in 1996.

Several key points support my coaching philosophy. First, as a coach you should not expect your athletes to do anything that you wouldn't do yourself. You should be a good role model to them; you must stay in shape. I've always tried to do that. I don't smoke, don't drink, and never got fat.

Setting an Example

I used to run every day, and I do mean *every* day. I had 21 years and 24 days of running without a break when I had to stop in 1994. I'd been running on a bad leg for the last three years and finally went to see my friend Dr. John Durkin. "If you continue to run," he told me, "you're going to be a cripple." So I had to quit.

But I've still never missed a day of teaching or coaching in 40 years. If I expect the kids to be there, I have to be there. I've never been late for practice in all that time. If I expect the kids to be on time, how can I be tardy?

1996 Captain Dave Walters and Mike Lucchesi award fellow senior, Pete Shin, the conference plaque for being a role model and an inspiration.

I've always tried to be the best I can be. If I expect the kids to excel, then I must do my best too. I've always been enthusiastic. If I expect the runners to be that way, I have to show enthusiasm myself. It's not an act. If it were, the kids would see through me in a minute.

I love my job and love the kids. I don't "work," but get paid for doing something I love. If my health stays good, I want to keep coaching until the year 2000. I'll be 71 then and will have coached in six decades and two centuries. How many people can say that?

Another way in which you act as a role model is with your work ethic. If you expect the runners to train both in season and out of season, you need to work the same way. How much of the year do I devote to cross country? Well, let's start with the season. That's three months. Then we're out training in November and December. That's five months total.

We have four months of track, in which the cross country runners compete. This brings us up to nine months. Finally we have three months of summer training (which is allowed in our state but not everywhere). So you see, I'm working with athletes the whole year.

Some people tell me, "You're killing these guys. They need a break." Yeah, I'm killing them right to the top of the mountain. They don't get there by taking breaks, and they know it. Their coach knows it too.

DEVELOPING ENTHUSIASM

As coaches you are primarily teachers. You exist to teach and train the athletes who come under your leadership, and what you do on the field, in the locker rooms, and in the classrooms may have implications weeks, months,

Concentration and commitment are vital to winning a cross country meet.

and even years later in the lives of your athletes. This is a sobering responsibility.

Yet I know of very few coaches—very few teachers—who do not accept this responsibility willingly and gladly. Indeed, coaches constantly work toward inspiring their athletes—their *students*, if you will—and exerting an influence that will, as educator Henry Adams said of the teacher, "affect eternity; he can never tell where his influence stops."

Enthusiasm is the key factor in all inspiration. If someone is enthusiastic about something—anything—this is communicated to those around him. If the enthusiastic person is on fire, you cannot help but feel the heat. How do you become enthusiastic? I feel it is a three-part process:

1. *You learn it.* Know all you can about your subject matter. Understand the sport and all its complexities.

2. *You love it.* Become convinced of the value and necessity of what you are teaching your athletes. See it as a joy rather than a task.
3. *You live it.* Bring your enthusiasm out to the field. Share your personal joy in your subject with those you instruct.

If you learn it, love it, and live it, if you believe these things, if you act upon them, then you cannot help but communicate your enthusiasm to your students, and they cannot help but be affected by it.

DEVELOPING BETTER HUMANS

I believe that the main role of athletics is to help our student-athletes be better humans. It's my hope that the athletes who pass through our program develop in the following ways.

1. They understand that success is being the best they can be every day they get up.
2. They develop a love of the sport, or at least an understanding and appreciation of it.
3. They leave our program with a good work ethic, a feeling that things worth having are worth working hard for.
4. They learn to work with others in a positive manner, even though they may not always like the people they are working with. In other words, treat others as you want them to treat you.
5. They leave the program with a good feeling about themselves and what they have accomplished in their time with us.

Chapter 2

COMMUNICATING YOUR APPROACH

A coach is a teacher, and a teacher is above all a communicator. Even if you work as a coaching staff of one, you don't work alone. You must communicate your own knowledge and commitment and your team's traditions and missions to many people.

You deal regularly with the athletes now on your team, of course, but also with would-be runners you're trying to recruit and with loyal alumni who continue to follow the team's fortunes. You work with other coaches–assistants if you're lucky enough to have them and surely those from competing schools. You cooperate with your school's administration and faculty, and with the student body at large. You talk with runners' parents, with community leaders, and with the media.

Chapter 1 encouraged you to clarify the message you want to deliver to and about your team. Now you will learn ways to spread that word. Yet another definition of communicator is "salesperson." You need to find effective ways to sell your cross country program.

COMMUNICATING WITH ATHLETES

When I was at Northwestern University, the only time we ever had a team meeting was when we were going on a trip. There was little sense of team, little of the bonding that I had known and loved in high school. So when I started coaching, I made a commitment to having *daily* meetings. It's the key to team-building and communication with the athletes.

Your most direct form of communication occurs at each day's practice, in the way you talk with your athletes. You have to take the attitude that everyone is important, because your team is only as strong as its weakest link.

This explains my policy against cutting anyone from the team. Everyone who comes to practice every day on time and gives their best effort stays on the team, whether they're the first runner or the 100th. We try to accomplish three things each day at practice to maintain a personal touch:

1. I take roll every single day. I don't let a manager do it; I take care of this myself. I want to let the runners know that I know they're at practice every day.

2. I call everyone's name out at least once during practice every day. I want everyone to know that I know they're running.

3. I make every runner come over at the end of practice and say, "I'm checking out, Mr. Newton." I want the runners to know that I appreciate their effort, so I make a point of shaking their hand—literally a personal touch.

I want every runner to feel special, so each one of them has a nickname. Instead of just being Smith and Jones, they're "Meatball" and "Hambone."

Calling Names

My practice of nicknaming athletes goes back to 1963. That year we had 25 freshmen, and a kid named Gus Milinka was 25th man. He was 6-3 and about 170, and he ran in gangly style. His technique was awful. Every day at practice I called him

York's J.V. women at the 1992 St. Charles Invitational.

"Milinkoff." I'd yell, "Milinkoff, you're looking great."

After that season he moved to Florida. A year later I got a letter from him saying, "I really miss being on the cross country team at York, and here's why. I know I was the worst runner on the team, but your telling me that I looked great and calling me by a nickname made my day." This kid opened my eyes. After that I really got serious about calling names.

The nicknames create a special bond between me and the kids, making each one different from anyone else. By the time they get to be juniors and seniors, they answer roll call with their nicknames. Years later I receive letters signed with the names that were given them.

It's no problem to remember the names and nicknames of everyone on the team. In fact, I can recall the names, nicknames, and times of athletes from 35 years ago. But if my wife asks me to pick up a loaf of bread on the way home from practice, I'll forget it. You remember the important things in your life.

It's my business to remember names; people want to hear them. I work at learning the names of everyone I associate with in my profession. It takes me about a week to identify everyone on the team each year, but once a name is in my memory bank it stays there.

COMMUNICATING WITH THE TEAM

Team meetings are essential. How else can you let everyone know at the same time what we're doing?

Except in summer when we're not working together every day, I don't hand out printed workout schedules for the day, week, or season. I don't want the runners asking me in advance, "What's the workout going to be, Mr. Newton?" They should be thinking about other things during the school day, like their classes,

without worrying about their upcoming workouts.

Besides, the veterans on the team already have a good idea what we're going to do. The pattern of workouts doesn't change much from year to year. If these runners kept a diary in the past, as I strongly encourage them to do, they already have a rough idea what we will run that day.

The diary is optional, and it's personal. The only reason I would check it is if something happens to runners and they go downhill. Then we analyze the diary to see what happened. Probably only about 20 percent of my runners keep diaries, however. But that's fine, because it's more important that the *coach* keep voluminous records, which I do.

The team learns the specifics of each day's training at the team meetings. We actually have *two* of these each day, one for what we call the "early shift" and another for the group that starts practice an hour later. We meet for 10 or 15 minutes. During this time we have the roll call, talk about the training that day (including why we're doing it and what its benefits will be), and anything else we need to discuss (such as travel plans for the upcoming meet).

Kids used to just do the workouts blindly. Now everyone questions everything. I know why we are doing particular workouts, so why not tell the athletes? Every workout should serve a purpose, and the runners deserve to know what that is so they will have confidence in the program.

COMMUNICATING IN PRIVATE

Coaching isn't limited to the hours of practice and meets. A coach should be available to talk with an athlete anytime.

If runners have problems, I'm as near as my office. They know they're always free to come and see me. My door is open, or they can stop and talk with me in the hallway at school. The runners know too that they are free to call me at home. But this very rarely happens, because the communication is so open and available at school.

The Illinois state meet awards assembly is always packed full of screaming York fans.

Along the same lines, if I really need to chew someone out, this is always done in private. You can yell at runners and correct them at practice, but you can't demean them in front of their teammates. Even in private I try to be constructive in my criticism. The two of us try to work out the problem in a positive way.

Talking It Out

Most of the private conferences involve kids from divorced families who live with one parent or the other. There's lots of animosity, lots of tension. The kids might not be coming to school or not doing their homework. They're on the wrong track because of the breakdown in the family.

For instance, I often have to talk with a kid whose weekend visits with an out-of-town parent conflict with our practice and meet schedules. Believe me, it isn't easy to tell someone, "We need you here, so you can't see Dad that day."

I counsel these kids, give them some TLC because they might not get enough of it at home. I'm not just a coach anymore but also a surrogate parent and an amateur psychologist. This has been a major adjustment for me.

COMMUNICATING IN WRITING

Coaches need to put something in writing, something for their runners to read later and maybe even to hang onto permanently as a memento. This can be as simple as a few pages or as elaborate as a thick book.

When starting to coach, I put out a summary book at the end of each season. The first year it was only five or six pages, then it grew by leaps and bounds from there. It's now over 250 pages. It contains the result of every runner in every meet, plus a historical record of other great York teams that have gone before. The kids devour this book, studying the names of runners on other teams as well as their own. This motivates them from one season to the next.

In addition they receive a preseason book (see figure 2.1). This baby gets thicker every year, now weighing in at more than 400 pages. The purpose of this book is to tell the athletes everything they need to know about cross country: the rules of the team, the meet schedule, what the courses are like, how their parents and friends can get to them, what it takes to win a letter, why we train as we do, and all sorts of other material.

About 300 pages of this preseason book is motivational material—inspirational sayings and stories, that sort of thing. The kids take it home and read it on their own, and pass it along to their parents if they wish. These books are part of my overall philosophy about communication: The athletes always know where they stand with me, exactly what I expect from them, and exactly what they can expect from me.

COMMUNICATING WITH PARENTS

The coach and the parents work as a team with the athlete. Everyone must work together.

Our school requires that in each sport we have a preseason meeting with the parents and athletes. We have ours on a morning of the first week of school, and we get about 95 percent attendance. We talk about team goals and rules, the training program, the meet schedule, the booster club, and similar matters.

Our preseason booklet also helps communicate what we're trying to do. If there are any problems with parents, they usually come when runners are new to our program. They aren't accustomed to working hard, to showing up every day on time, or to following our other rules. They come home tired, sore, and complaining. Parents then call me to ask, "What's going on here?"

I have a standard answer to that. I say, "Cross country is one of the most tiring sports, but you should be happy about that. You have your kid home, resting, instead of out on the street corner looking for trouble. Be patient, and you'll see the payoff for this hard training." Actually we get very few calls from parents, because the workouts are so easy in the beginning.

If the kids stay with the program, the parents eventually see how much good it's doing them. The calls from concerned parents usually stop after runners have been on the team for awhile. As a group our parents are marvelous. We get such great support from them that they are sometimes called my "entourage." People whose kids ran for me 25 years ago come out to the meets and volunteer to drive to the meets or help conduct them.

The parents have an unofficial boosters club for our cross country team. Their activities include an annual Labor Day picnic at the start of each season and a party for the team when it returns from the state meet. Our parent support is second to none. We couldn't achieve what we do without this teamwork.

COMMUNICATING WITH ALUMNI

The alumni can be a great source of support for the current team. Having them come back to watch meets and to continue participating in other ways gives the program a sense of continuity.

We promote this participation with an Alumni Run on Labor Day weekend each year. The current team has a time trial the same day as the alums run a separate race, which has been a tradition for more than 35 years. Jeff O'Rourke, who was a student manager at York in the early 1980s, still handles the correspondence with the

1996 YORK CROSS COUNTRY

Coach Joe Newton

"The Long Green Line"

National Champions | 1974,75,76,77,78,79,80,81,82,83,84,85,86,
89,90,91,95

State Champions | 1962,65,68,71,72,73,78,80,81,82,84,86,89,
90,91,92,93,94

WSC Champions | 1962,63,64,65,66,67,68,69,71,72,73,74,75,
76,77,78,79,80,81,82,83,84,85,86,87,88,89,
90,91,92,93,94,95

Figure 2.1 1996 preseason book cover.

MEN of 1996 we are now down at the bottom of the mountain looking up. The "LONG GREEN LINE" is back to square one. Our streak has ended and we have no where to go but UP. Our DESTINY is now in your hands. We must pull ourselves up by the bootstraps and go on from here. As you think about the monumental task that faces us I want you to remember the common phenomenon in psychology called the PLACEBO effect. It means that if you are convinced something will happen, you will unconsciously MAKE it happen. To further illustrate my point, Golfer Dave Stockton was once asked at the start of the Masters' Tournament to name the player he most feared in that field of golf champions. "Me," he answered without hesitation. No one else has ever stated more succinctly the truth that it's what goes on INSIDE you that counts most in athletic performance.

WE'RE GOING TO WIN . . . . YOU BELIEVE THAT!!!!!

Crystal Lake Central, Lockport, Schaumburg, Marist, Naperville North, Fenton, and Naperville Central all will have GREAT teams and will do anything to beat York. You are the BENCHMARK that all other teams use to compare their programs. So what makes York stand out when the general makeup of all teams is about the same? Our secret at York is very simple and it's centered around 2 words that add deeply to any natural talent that you might possess. The magical words are DESIRE and CONFIDENCE. Desire is the drive for success. This striving for excellence allows you to "DO THE BEST YOU CAN WITH WHAT YOU GOT." Confidence is a belief in your ability. It is having faith in your talents and accepting all challenges that test your limits.

WE'RE GOING TO WIN . . . . YOU BELIEVE THAT!!!!!

We only have TWO men returning from your 1995 team. They both know what it will take to win. They know for us to go back to the top of the mountain they must provide strong leadership. That leadership will lead to great chemistry, that in turn will lead to CONSISTENCY in practice on a daily basis.

WE'RE GOING TO WIN . . . . YOU BELIEVE THAT!!!!!

My true goal for this team is to start a STREAK OF 1. To do that we will need a maximum performance from each and every one of you. Remember, we are only as strong as our weakest link. If we all focus and concentrate on the task at hand then SYNERGY will kick in and amazing things will happen!

WE'RE GOING TO WIN . . . . YOU BELIEVE THAT!!!!!

Our mission for the 1996 season is to bring York back to where it deserves to be #1. . . . We must re-establish our INVINCIBILITY. We will do this in three ways. First by being ASSERTIVE . . . that means you will take appropriate risks to be successful. Second by PERSONAL ACCOUNTABILITY . . . which means you are responsible for your actions, having a willingness to face up to your shortcomings and to pay the price of trying to correct them. Third by SELF-DISCIPLINE . . . which means you are willing to develop and then stick to your personal "GAME PLAN." Remember to take a psychological risk every time you compete. You risk looking foolish, losing to someone you shouldn't, disappointing yourself, coaches, parents, and friends—losing prestige. My response to you is we need runners who view pressure and crises as challenges, not threats, as opportunities to test yourselves under difficult conditions. You must go well beyond simply loving to win. You must come to enjoy battle, to enjoy the challenges that York cross country poses. You can't fear nervousness. You want to be nervous. That's the idea. That makes it fun, it allows you to do great things if you let it. Our theme for 1996: "#20 WILL BE AS SWEET AS HONEY."

Joseph Newton
Head Cross Country Coach

Figure 2.2 Coach Newton's 1996 preseason letter.

Alumni come to Elmhurst's East End Park for York's annual Alumni Day. This has been a long-standing York tradition.

alumni. He sends out letters to hundreds of them.

About 100 turn out for the run, with about half of them competing and the others coming just for the reunion. They run our old 1.8-mile course, and the race can get quite competitive. Just before the Alumni Run I introduce each of the alums by what they did while they were in school. The current kids know the old-timers' names, and this lets them put a body and face with the legend.

We also send the graduates a schedule of each year's meets, asking them to come out and cheer. Many of them travel to the state meet itself and talk to the team before the race. They talk about how it was for them at State. The current kids think, "We better not let them down." They see that they're running for more than themselves.

COMMUNICATING WITH ASSISTANTS

Coaches who say they don't need help are kidding themselves. I never had any full-time assistants for cross country, and only occasionally has a student teacher volunteered to help out. Another coach would be a godsend in some ways.

This is especially true with the two-shift setup we use, with two groups starting practice about an hour apart. I have to break away from the first shift's workout to take roll and have a team meeting for the second. Sometimes it's exasperating. An assistant might take over that first workout until I got back. On the other hand I like working alone. As Frank Sinatra sang, I like doing it my way.

My secret weapon is our student managers. That's why one coach can handle more than 100 runners each year. Our team couldn't function without them. We have more managers at York than most teams have runners. Typically they number about 10, with each having a specific role.

Two work strictly on computers, compiling results and the other material for our preseason and postseason booklets. One videotapes the meets, and another is the still photographer. Then there's one who only records all the times on a clipboard. Several of them know how to use a stopwatch and do the timing. As a special reward we take two or three of the student managers to the state meet.

I recruit the managers the same way as runners—from the gym classes. I tell them, "You get to be part of the team and don't have to run a step." We have no shortage of volun-

teers. They like to be around winners, and they're treated well.

COMMUNICATING WITH THE SCHOOL

Here's a tip for young coaches: When you have a lot of success in any high school athletic program, about 90 percent of the staff at school tends to resent you.

We try to defuse this by involving a large number of staff people in putting on meets. We'll have math or English teachers out as officials. When they're involved, their resentment vanishes. They now feel part of the team and understand what we're trying to accomplish. Coaches in other sports might also resent you if you don't support their programs in return. So I make a point of helping

The backbone of any championship team: the managers. Ian Vertovec, Eric Neubauer, Mike Lioni, Matt McGrath, and Brian Margner watch as the race unfolds.

out at swimming and wrestling meets and at football and basketball games.

Along these same lines, support from the school administration, both from the overall school administrator and from the athletic director, is essential. Fortunately it's first-rate on both counts at York. If the principal doesn't actually attend the state meet, he's at the school to greet us when we come home. He's wonderful to me, allowing time off for speaking engagements because he feels I'm representing the school there.

As for dealing with the athletic director, this is easy. His name is Al Janulis, and he started running for me in the eighth grade. He eventually ran a 48-second quarter mile and was captain of Northwestern's track team. Our program obviously has his full blessing.

Generating Support

Ideally your school will treat cross country as the major sport that you coaches like to think it is. At York this truly happens. We get crowds of 500 to 600 at dual meets, and about 2,000 fans follow us to the state meet. At the awards ceremony half the crowd is from York and half from the other 26 schools.

We have cheerleaders at all the meets, and the band goes with us to State. I always make a point of telling them, "Your cheering and playing were worth 30 points to us." When we come home from winning a state meet, 200 to 300 cars parade through downtown. A crowd of 1,000 to 1,500 greets us in the gym, and we have an all-school assembly the next week.

Every November the York band goes down to Peoria to support their cross country team.

Three people in particular are responsible for this tremendous support: Al Janulis, our athletic director; Jan Jumper, who's in charge of cheerleaders (and has the perfect name for it!); and Ron Polancich, the band director at York. Without them, the level of enthusiasm at our school wouldn't be what it is.

COMMUNICATING WITH THE MEDIA

Another key to a successful program is how you're treated by the media. Coaches make the mistake of thinking that coverage comes automatically. It doesn't. You have to cultivate it. No matter how tired you are or how late it is when you come back from a meet, you must call in the results to the media.

I call reporters all the time because the kids want to see their names in the paper, and so do their parents and friends, and this isn't going to happen by osmosis. I talk to reporters constantly. I'm never too busy to talk to them, knowing what they can do for us and our sport.

Cross country gets great coverage in the Chicago area, and this doesn't come by pure luck. The coaches made it happen.

COMMUNICATING WITH COACHES

I've learned after 40-plus years in this profession that everyone loves you when you're a loser. When you beat them, everything changes. Other coaches start sniping at you. You have to decide: Are you going to be a loser and have everyone like you, or a winner and some people resent you? I made my choice and am willing to live with the consequences.

Let me add, though, that the vast majority of my dealings with other coaches are positive. We correspond and talk on the phone, and we meet at coaching clinics where I speak. Most coaches want to learn from someone who knows how to win.

Coaching Coaches

One of the most gratifying aspects of my career is seeing how many former York athletes have gone into coaching. I can think of at least 20, and some of them love having a chance to knock off their old coach.

Pete Reiff was the captain on our 1968 state championship cross country team. He now coaches at Hoffman Estates High School, we run against him often, and his teams are always competitive and always out to beat ours.

Two other former York runners now coach at the college level: Bruce Coleman at the University of Wisconsin/Oshkosh, and Bob Schultz at Elmhurst College. I'd like nothing better than to send athletes on to Bruce or Bob, knowing they'd be in good hands.

Chapter 3

MOTIVATING RUNNERS

Motivation starts at the top. Of course it literally starts there—in the mind—first as a dream, then a plan, then a commitment to carry it through. But it also begins with the *head coach*, who shares the dream, makes the plan, and builds the competitive fire in athletes to reach the goals they've set.

Motivating can be a tricky job in cross country, a difficult sport offering little apparent glory, at least not at first when a program is building. Runners do most of their competing apart from cheering crowds. They compete for media attention, usually unsuccessfully, against King Football, which shares the autumn season. Coaches also compete for talent and school attention with the increasingly popular soccer and volleyball.

The motivation to run well in cross country comes from the athlete as an individual, from the team as a group, and from the coach as a leader. Whole books have been written on this subject (including one of my own). Here I'll summarize the motivational techniques that have proven effective with my team.

MOTIVATING YOURSELF

Just as athletes must set goals for themselves, so must the coach. Aristotle said that life is only meaningful if you're striving for a goal. Fortunately I've always been a very goal-oriented person. As noted earlier, one of my goals is still to be coaching in the year 2000. Another is to coach York to 20 state cross country titles; we're one away from that as I write this page.

These goals—always striving for something, always doing the best I can—keep up my enthusiasm. This is what gets me up at four o'clock every morning. This is what keeps me working out. Though I can't run anymore, it's still possible to ride a bike and lift weights.

It keeps me young and excited to touch the lives of these young people. It's tremendously rewarding to see them grow from young, awkward, vacillating freshmen into fit, confident, disciplined members of a winning team. The kids raise my spirits more than I raise theirs.

My basic message in talks to coaches is, if you aren't motivated, how can you expect your runners to be? Enthusiasm plus care will motivate any young athlete, while lack of excitement and concern on your part will kill any kid's interest.

Coaches ask me, "Why can't we win? We do the workouts in the books." Well, there's a lot more to winning than workouts. You can't win just by reading the training books. You have to pay just as much attention, if not more, to the mental and emotional aspects of the sport. Your team has to be mentally prepared for workouts and, especially, for meets.

You coaches know you've succeeded as a motivator when every runner on your team

The 1992 men of York pose in their tuxedos after winning the state championship for the fourth consecutive year.

does not want to lose for fear of hurting your feelings. And you don't want to lose for fear of hurting *their* feelings. That's how much you care about each other and what you're all doing.

Caring and Sharing

At the 1970 state meet York finished seventh. We were sitting in the bleachers at the awards ceremony, and I was feeling really melancholy. Jon Woods, one of our runners, said, "Don't feel bad, Mr. Newton. We let you down. It was our fault."

I could have told him and the other runners the same thing: It was my fault for not preparing them well enough for this meet. They shouldn't feel bad, because I'd let them down. That's when I realized we were doing something right. This incident showed how much we cared about each other and what we were all doing.

MOTIVATING WITH REWARDS

A coach must be both a butt-kicker and a back-patter, or what I like to call a "benevolent dictator." You're the boss. You must take charge of the team. Kids want direction and discipline. But they also want to be told that they've done a good job. They want someone to pick them up when they're down. I chew people out and also hug them. They always know exactly how I feel.

You must also establish an extensive reward system. Awards of all types are great

The 1996 York women with Olympic champion Michael Johnson.

motivators for young runners. They scrape and scratch to win them.

We give all types of awards within our team. These start with T-shirts for the 1,000-mile club, given to anyone who runs that much mileage during the summer months. Runners can also win 2,000- and 3,000-mile shirts for consecutive thousand-mile summers.

In our first intrasquad meet of the fall we award T-shirts saying "York Top 12." The runners who wear these will change as the season goes along. Runners can literally take the shirt off others' backs by pushing them out of the top 12.

High school athletes strive to be letterwinners. I purposely set the standards low for winning a letter so everyone can get one. These runners work hard all season and deserve this honor that everyone in school recognizes.

Within our team we give dozens of awards at a special ceremony the Thursday before the state meet. These include the Gold Brick Award, given to the team's biggest screw-off. These awards, handed out by the team captains, give many of the lesser runners who don't normally get prizes the chance to win something.

Matt Murray displays a short haircut, an old tradition at York.

MOTIVATING WITH RULES

Rules should be few but ironclad. The athletes shouldn't have the slightest doubt what the rules are or what will happen if they don't abide by them. No one, athlete or parent, should have any doubt about these rules. We give them by the eyes and the ears, in writing and at the early meetings, so ignorance of the rules is no excuse.

Come to all practices on time, no smoking, no drinking, no drugs. Break any of these and a runner is off the team, simple as that. Academically, if they're flunking a class two weeks in a row they're off the team. My rule here is stiffer than the school's policy for other athletes. "You're a *student*-athlete," I tell my kids. "The word 'student' comes first. Your number one function here is to get grades."

Making No Exceptions

We have fewer than 10 rules, but we live and die by those. Anyone who is expelled from the team can't come back until next year. We make no exceptions for the top athletes.

One year my number one runner came late to practice by an hour. I said that's it, you're done. This was his senior year, and he never came back. The other kids were shocked, but this was an important lesson to them: no exceptions, period.

A coach named Bruce Waha told me at a clinic way back in 1961, "No matter who you kick off your team, there will be someone to replace him. Someone will step up." I've always found that to be true.

The 1989 state championship. "How sweet it is!"

Our team rules are simple. All runners understand that this is expected of them of as a minimum:

1. Runners on the early shift are expected to be suited up and on the field by 2:35 P.M. Runners on the second shift are expected to be suited up and on the field by 3:30 P.M.

2. Roll will be taken by me each day. *Runners must check in with me* before practice and *out with me* before they leave.

3. If they report late, they must submit a note from the teacher who detained them showing the time they were dismissed. They must report suited up 20 minutes after the time indicated on the note. *There are no exceptions.* The second time runners are late without a note, they will be dismissed from the squad.

4. The only legitimate excuse from practice is absence from school. When runners return, they bring their admit to prove their absence. *An unsatisfactory readmit will result in dismissal from the squad.* If runners are in school and out of practice twice (two unexcused absences), they will be dismissed from the squad. If they are kept for detention or a meeting, they are not excused from practice. They are expected to bring a note from the detention supervisor or teacher and be suited up 20 minutes after the detention or meeting is completed.

5. Runners must be academically eligible. Eligibility is checked every week and is based on their record in class from the beginning of the semester. Anyone ineligible for more than one week will be dismissed from the squad. The reason for this is that, if they are ineligible, they cannot compete and we cannot depend on them. If they can't clear up their work with a teacher in a week, they are indicating poor interest in the team. We can't use them with that attitude. Runners are expected to work out during their ineligible period.

6. Anyone using alcohol or tobacco is not interested in athletics and will be dismissed from the squad. No training rule is violated more than the no-smoking edict, but if runners aren't strong enough to resist, or smart enough to stay away from this and other drugs, they'll never be the athletes we want.

7. Keeping late hours results in dismissal. Hours are as follows: Sunday through Thursday, 10:00 P.M.; Friday or Saturday, 12:30 A.M. (If they take a 12:30 A.M. one night, we expect runners in early by 10:00 P.M. the other night.) Rest is essential!

8. Runners cannot play intramurals if they are on the cross country team.

MOTIVATING EVERYONE

The bigger your team, the greater this problem will be. Only seven runners get to compete in the state meet, and on our team this means more than 100 stand by and watch.

"We all win together," I tell our team. "Everyone made a contribution by coming out to practice all year, by running the other meets, and by pushing the top seven." Another of our rewards, if we win the state meet, is to give patches to everyone on the varsity. Same with the conference meet if we win there.

Keep in mind that all the athletes get to run in most of the meets. In Illinois we have three levels in dual meets: freshman, sophomore, and varsity. A team may enter an unlimited number of runners at each of these levels. At invitationals the levels change slightly: usually seven varsity runners and seven sophomores, with the freshmen and junior varsity races unlimited.

This isn't football or basketball, volleyball or soccer. No one languishes on the bench all year or gets cut from the team in cross country. Knowing they'll compete regularly is another motivator.

Cross country is an unusual sport in that the athletes both work together as a team and compete against each other as individuals.

Marius Bakken winning the 1995 Lyons regional. He missed Jim Spivey's course record by one second.

We promote a spirit of friendly competition within the team. We divide our cross country squad into six groups. I'll call Group One the "Magnificent Seven," Group Two the "Emerging Seven," Group Three the "Developing Seven," and so on. Group Five has 15 to 20 runners, and Group Six maybe 40. In addition there are two freshman groups.

Each group has a captain whose job is to make the runners work harder. Changes take place all year in the makeup of these groups. The athletes take great pride in moving up.

I tell the captains to lead by example. They don't have to be loud, but they have to fight against peer-group pressure to let people slack off. It's a tough job being a captain, and I pick runners who've shown they can handle it.

Leading From Within

My captains don't need to be the Most Valuable Performers on the team, only the Most Valuable *People*. Two of the all-time greatest captains at York didn't even make the top seven runners and didn't get to compete in the state meet.

Joe Wagner was the last of four brothers who ran for me. All of them ran at State except Joe. He was our 10th man as a senior, yet he was the captain—and a tremendous one. He worked hard, and everyone respected him.

James Sheridan (who wrote the letter that opens part III of this book) loved to run. He was one of our slowest freshmen but moved up to ninth man as a senior. I made him the captain even though we had one of the best runners in the country that year.

MOTIVATING BY EMPOWERMENT

The new buzzword going around these days is "empowerment." You need to understand what this word means and then employ it with your team. Trying to give a clear, precise definition is elusive, but basically it refers to making the team *theirs*. This means the team members adopt the coach's vision of a successful team, making it their personal cause, and use all their talents to make the vision come true.

We have been doing this for more than 40 years at York High School, but until recently I never knew that it had a name. Now we realize it's "empowerment." If you are going to empower your athletes, you must give much time and thought to the selection of captains. This is the key to making this concept work.

We make being a captain of a York cross country team a very special honor. I emphasize that only a special few are chosen, and once they are they must step up and accept the responsibilities that the job entails. Initially I pick the captains. We have many of them in order to pass around the leadership

role. For instance, we name a different captain for each meet.

In practice we assign a different captain to each of our six training groups. He must be a strong leader who will pull the group up to his level rather than going down to theirs. Our team captains have other duties. These include selecting a team motto for the year, naming award-winners for the season, designing a T-shirt for the state meet, and picking tuxes for the team to wear at that meet.

Athletes who are empowered are not just carrying out the wishes of the coach and the captains, but they have bought into the team concept. They have made it a personal challenge to do their best for *their* team.

MOTIVATING MIGHTY MITES

Maybe five times in 40 years I've encountered runners who were *too* motivated for their own good. They worked too hard in training or psyched themselves out at races. Far more often a coach runs into the opposite problem—the runner with talent who doesn't want to do anything.

Once in a blue moon you find someone who has talent *and* wants to work. Then you really have something. But you can't sit back and wait for a star like this to come along. You must work with what you have.

Only 3 percent of high school runners will ever compete in college, and only 1 percent of those ever make it to the top there. You're better off concentrating on the mighty mites. These are the ones who might run 10-minute two miles after working their butts off for four years. Put together five of those and you have a winning team.

Brian Gary finishing the 1994 state cross country meet, leading to our sixth straight state championship.

My First Mighty Mite

My very first mighty mite was Gary Goss, who came into the program in 1963 as a four-foot-eight freshman. He grew to about 5-2 by the time he was a senior. I have a picture of him in my first book, *The Long*

Green Line, noting that he has perfect running form.

Gary still contributes heavily to our program by conducting all of our home meets (see chapter 11) . He also does the timing at many road races in the area and runs some of them. Gary grew into our mightiest mite of all.

MOTIVATING WITH RESPECT

Successful motivation should be based on the psychological laws of learning. Young people learn to follow patterns that produce results that are satisfactory to them.

Young people need to be motivated, not only to produce in athletics but also to exhibit self-discipline and responsible behavior. They need to be motivated to face the challenges and obligations of living. They must learn the art of self-control. They should be equipped with the personal strength needed to meet the demands imposed on them by their school, coach, peer group, and community.

There are those who believe that such characteristics cannot be taught (motivated). They say that the best you can do is send your athletes down the path of least resistance, as you sweep aside any hurdles they might encounter. The advocates of this laissez-faire philosophy would recommend that kids be allowed to fail in school, on the field, in the home, and anywhere else. In other words, let your athletes "do their own thing."

I reject this notion and have accumulated considerable evidence to refute it. Permissiveness has not been a failure; it has been a disaster. Kids thrive best in a coaching situation that has an atmosphere of genuine love, undergirded by reasonable, consistent discipline and enthusiastic motivation. Jack London wrote, "The best measurement of anything should be: does it work?" Motivation, as I practice it, works.

The key to motivation is mutual respect. If you want the young athletes on your team to respect you, you must respect them. The only

Jim Mallaney finishing strong in the 1997 WSC meet.

way this can happen is if you apply equal amounts of love and discipline. Then the motivation will naturally fall into place.

MOTIVATING FOR LIFE

This list is adapted and expanded from one originally compiled by Harry Schneider, coach of the Middle Country cross country team at Centereach High School, New York.

1. Compliment three people every day.
2. Watch a sunrise at least once a year.
3. Have a firm handshake.
4. Look people in the eye.
5. Say "thank you" a lot; write thank-you notes promptly.
6. Take time to listen to your favorite music all alone once each week.
7. Sing along with songs that you like.

8. Stand at attention and put your hand over your heart when singing the National Anthem.
9. Learn to identify the music of Chopin, Mozart, and Beethoven.
10. Be the first to say "hello."
11. Return all things you borrow.
12. Treat everyone you meet like you want to be treated.
13. Keep secrets.
14. Never give up on anyone.
15. Remember that miracles happen every day.
16. Show respect for teachers, for the police, and for your elders.
17. Don't waste time learning the "tricks of the trade"; instead learn the trade.
18. Control your temper.
19. Put the cap back on the toothpaste.
20. Take out the garbage without being told.
21. Enjoy beautiful things; always have something beautiful in sight.
22. Smile a lot; smile at someone once each hour for one full day.
23. Take responsibility for everything that you do or fail to do.
24. Accept a compliment with a simple "thank you."
25. Live so that when others think of fairness, caring, and integrity, they think of you.
26. Use your sense of humor to amuse, not abuse.
27. Dot your "i's" and cross your "t's."
28. Be brave; even if you're not, pretend to be, because no one can tell the difference.
29. Touch the ones you love.
30. Don't take good health and your body for granted.
31. Don't mess with drugs, alcohol, or smoking; enjoying life will give you everything the drugs could give you.
32. Avoid sarcastic remarks.
33. Earn trust, and learn to trust.
34. Slow dance.
35. Refill ice-cube trays.
36. Choose your friends carefully; you will influence each other greatly.
37. Make it a habit to do nice things for people who'll never find out.
38. Don't miss class.
39. Think big thoughts, but relish small pleasures.
40. Go for a walk alone at least once a week.
41. Never cheat.
42. Put a marshmallow in your hot chocolate.
43. Learn CPR.
44. Learn to listen; opportunity sometimes knocks very softly.
45. Know how to tie a tie.
46. Remember people's names.
47. When people are relating an important event that happened to them, don't try to top them with a story of your own; let them have the stage.
48. Be on time.
49. Never deprive someone of hope; it might be all they have.
50. Strive for excellence, not perfection.
51. Avoid negative people.
52. Be neat.
53. Realize that the person with big dreams is more powerful than one with all the facts.
54. Be kinder than necessary.
55. Give people a second chance, but not a third.
56. Never take action when you're angry.
57. Battle against prejudice or discrimination wherever you find it.
58. Wear out, don't rust out.
59. Let people know what you stand for, and what you won't stand for.
60. Ask why.
61. Measure people by the size of their heart.
62. Become the most positive and enthusiastic person you know.
63. Have good posture.
64. Enter a room with purpose and confidence.
65. Don't forget, a person's greatest emotional need is to feel appreciated.
66. Show respect for all living things.
67. Loosen up, relax.

Phil Olson grinds to a halt in the chute of the 1996 Palatine Invitational.

68. Commit yourself to constant self-improvement.
69. Remember that being a good loser is different than not caring about losing.
70. Don't major in minor things.
71. Praise in public, criticize in private.
72. When someone hugs you, let him or her be the first to let go.
73. Know that good manners matter.
74. Keep your promises; promise and deliver.
75. Save some money each week.
76. Recognize that you only have one chance to make a first impression.
77. Respect tradition.
78. Wave to children on a school bus.
79. Show respect for others' time.
80. Hang out with people smarter than yourself.
81. Be modest; a lot was accomplished before you arrived.
82. Lie on your back and watch the clouds or the stars.
83. Remember that overnight success takes about three years.
84. Leave everything a little better than you found it.
85. Think of what you would change in yourself, then change it.
86. Realize how you affect others.
87. Practice empathy; try to see things from other people's point of view.
88. Learn to say "no" politely.
89. Don't expect life to be fair.
90. Never criticize others' family.
91. Never underestimate the power of forgiveness.
92. Don't say you don't have enough time; you have exactly the same number of hours as the rest of us do.
93. If you think you have no time to work out, do push-ups.

94. Remember that winners do what losers don't want to do.
95. Check the smoke detector's batteries.
96. Live your life with an *exclamation*, not an explanation.
97. Live so that when you look back on your life, you'll regret the things you *didn't* do more than those you did.
98. Never waste an opportunity to tell someone you love them.
99. Keep a dictionary on your desk at home.
100. Never eat the last cookie.
101. Be grateful and acknowledge those who help you.
102. Take charge of your attitude; don't let someone else choose it for you.
103. Pay attention to details.
104. Be a self-starter.
105. Pay your fair share.
106. Remain curious about your ability.
107. When attending meetings, sit up front.
108. Don't litter.
109. Don't flaunt your success, but don't apologize for it either.
110. Don't procrastinate; do it now.
111. Help out at the Special Olympics.
112. Always do more than the minimum, even if no one will know.
113. Waste no opportunities, because they can never be regained.
114. Ask yourself, "Will this help me become my very best?"
115. Become someone's hero.
116. Adopt the motto, "If it is to be, it is up to me."

Many tears were shed after the 1995 loss.

117. Remember that quitters never win and winners never quit.
118. Believe that the future belongs to those who prepare for it.
119. Assure success through persistence and determination.
120. Press on!

Chapter 4

BUILDING A CROSS COUNTRY PROGRAM

The best-laid plans for training and racing will go nowhere if you don't have the troops to carry them out. I intentionally use the army term because, as in the infantry, the "foot soldiers" of cross country must be recruited. You need to tap all available sources of recruits—the age-group running clubs, your school's track team, the gym classes, and the middle schools or junior highs. You need a steady stream of new runners from which to replace each year's graduates and build the current team.

You require a minimum of five runners to score as a team, and at least two more to fill out the team if one of the leaders should stumble. But I encourage you to think in terms of big numbers instead of small ones. The more athletes you recruit, the better. Think of the team as a pyramid. The wider its base in terms of numbers, the higher its peak will reach in terms of quality.

This chapter deals almost entirely with recruiting. With these ongoing efforts you build and maintain your program.

BUILDING A TEAM

Many coaches have the problem of recruiting enough runners to fill out their squad. But that's because they expect the runners to come to them. It doesn't usually happen that way. You have to go out and get them.

My first year at York we had about 20 runners on the team. That was a major jump from what they'd had before. They came out for the team because I recruited them. I went to every gym class and signed up as many as possible who weren't already committed to another fall sport. I was in a perfect position to do this, because I taught gym and saw these kids every day. It was hard at first; I'm not going to lie to you. But we established this recruiting system right away, and it has worked ever since.

You have to grab them right away. We focus on the first day of school, when only the freshmen attend and sample each class for just 13 minutes. We make sure they come to the gym. Fifteen of our top cross country runners wait there with clipboards. Whatever door the freshmen come in, a runner grabs them and asks if they're signed up for any fall sport.

If not, they get a one-minute recruiting pitch for cross country. We make sure they see all the state- and national-championship banners hanging in the gym. The team members get more recruits than I do. My job the next day is to go back to the freshman gym classes and catch them a second time, especially those who didn't show up for practice the first night.

Speaking of Recruiting

I have a standard speech that I've been giving for about 30 years. I tell stories about runners who didn't want to be at this meet-

Coach Newton during an interview with Continental Cablevision during the 1995 Alumni Meet at East End Park.

ing, then four years later were members of state championship teams. Then I'll point out someone in the gym and shout, "Shorty, you come with me, and I'll make you an All-Stater." The other kids are thinking, "If he can make Shorty an All-Stater, what can he do with me?" It's a selling job. If you just give a monotone talk, the kids will tune you out.

"Somebody lied to you," I say in my recruiting talk. "They said cross country was going to be hard. Well, all I ask you to do at first is run one lap around that track. That means you only practice for 90 seconds." The second thing I tell them is, "Somebody also lied to you when they said you had to be a good runner. You don't have to be good. We'll *make* you good."

I really mean it when I say that they don't need to be great athletes coming in. Some of the worst freshmen become the best seniors, while some of the best freshmen, including those who've competed

successfully in age-group running, don't stick around.

The whole program hinges on what happens that first couple of days of school. I come to school feeling sick with nervous tension, asking myself, "What if we don't get one new runner?" It's easier to find one good athlete if you have 50 or 100 freshmen than 2 or 3.

If you let down in recruiting one year, your whole program will suffer two or three years down the road. You have to sell your program. You have to recruit every year.

Building From the Bottom

We have no qualifying standards for joining the team. Setting a standard or holding a tryout would contradict the policy of opening

The York Dukes, at the 400-meter mark, race to get ahead of the pack at the 1996 state championship.

the team to everyone, regardless of ability. The new runners must only show an interest in the sport.

Showing Improvement

For several years I told the story of Jim Hackbarth to potential recruits. "When I recruited him in 1963," I tell them, "there were 25 freshmen. He was 25th. The next year he was only the 10th sophomore. But then as a junior he moved up to number three on the varsity, and as a senior he was the number one runner with the third fastest time in America that year for two miles on the track."

I added that Jim earned a full scholarship at Eastern Illinois University and while there was on teams that won two national championships in cross country. The speech ended with, "And now let me introduce you to Jim Hackbarth." Then this living legend came out in his letter sweater and gave a one-minute speech.

Sandra Meneses, 1995.

We break the recruits in gently. They don't run their first meet until they've practiced for about a month. Then they are required to satisfy one standard. We do not give freshmen a York uniform until they have earned it by running every step of their first race. We don't care if they finish dead last. If they run all the way, they get their team uniform the very next day.

Building From Within

The current athletes who help with the recruiting of new ones are a coach's greatest resource. They know many of the younger kids and how to speak their language.

We have a little contest to see who can recruit the most people. The veterans love this. All I have to do is give them a little session on what to say. "Don't try to intimidate anyone," I tell them. "Don't threaten anyone. Be positive." It's been a real pleasure to have the older runners do this. It shows them again that it's *their* team.

Building on Experience

The junior highs (middle schools) are not as big a resource as they might seem. The sixth-, seventh-, and eighth-graders here do compete in cross country, but we only get 10 or 15 of them each year. Many who ran in junior high go out for soccer or volleyball in high school because they didn't have that sport before. A cross country coach's biggest competition for athletes in the fall is soccer, which attracts the same type of kids as running does.

Also, the age-group track clubs in our area don't have much of an effect on the makeup of a team. There are youth clubs in the area, and some of the kids are quite talented. But this can be a mixed blessing. They might have had the devil worked out of them, and they're already tired of the sport when they start high school. Or they might have been so successful that they were flying to meets all over the country and getting first-class treatment wherever they went. It can be a letdown when they come to our program and have to ride in a rickety old school bus.

Building for Track

Some schools have no choice about using cross country as training for other sports, notably track. They have to fill out the squad any way they can. We have a choice, and we don't have to use anyone who isn't really into this sport. Cross country is such a serious sport here at York that everyone knows they're here to work hard for the meets in cross country season, not to get in shape for another sport later in the year.

My approach is that cross country is an entity unto itself, not a training ground for track. Runners who aren't trying to do their best in the fall might as well be playing football or soccer.

I realize that smaller schools don't have the luxury of numbers that we do at York. But in even the smallest schools you can usually find at least five people willing to run. This might involve selling them on the idea of using the cross country season to get in shape for basketball, which often is the big sport at small schools. You take whomever you can get.

Fielding a Team

My first job was at Waterman, Illinois, which had only about 50 kids in high school when I started the cross country team my second year there. Many of those kids already played baseball in the fall, and I talked some into doubling up in cross country during the same season. I grabbed a few more kids who were lounging around the hallways and a few more who were waiting for the basketball season to start.

We came out with a team of eight, and the amount of running they did was laughable by today's standards. But no one else in schools our size had many more runners than we did or worked any harder. Waterman's first-ever cross country team won the conference title.

Building by Numbers

Recruiting runners is only one part of your task. *Keeping* them is another. We keep almost 98 to 99 percent of our athletes from the top three classes from the beginning to the end of the season, and about 75 percent of the freshmen.

Some of these are lost to injury, a few for the season but most for only a few days. We call the casualties our "Hospital Corps." It will

At each state meet, Andy Barrett is the official team spirit leader for the York team area.

number five to eight on a typical day. Our injury rate is small. In all my years at York we've only had a couple of runners who weren't healthy on the day of the state meet.

The size of our team might sound unbelievable to some of you. But remember that we took a while to get this big. We started the most recent year with 189 kids signed up (this from a student body of about 1,900). The majority of them, 107, were freshmen. Of those freshmen, 20 never came to practice after indicating an interest. About 20 more quit after the first week of bare-minimum training, saying it was "too time-consuming" or "too exhausting." If we started them out hard, we'd have *nobody* left.

We shook out at 135 on the full team. Of these 27 were seniors, 24 juniors, 21 sophomores, and 63 freshmen. My plan is to keep 50 freshmen through the first year. Then, if 25 of

them come back the next season and at least 15 of them run until they are seniors, we have experienced runners at the top each season.

Gaining Experience

Our top seven runners in 1996 consisted of four seniors, two juniors, and one freshman. It's quite rare for a freshman to make our varsity team. It has happened only twice before, and those two became our all-time superstars. Jim White ran a 4:07 mile and Ron Craker an 8:51 two-mile in high school, and both went on to compete for Indiana University.

Our 1996 freshman was Donald Sage Jr. His father, Donald Sr., had been a great miler at Northern Illinois University and

Rob McMonigle leads the 1995 race in Schaumburg.

was a high school coach for many years. Young Donald started running with his dad when he was a little bitty guy, but Dad never let him overwork and burn out.

Donald Jr. began running with me in our summer program as a sixth-grader. So even though he was just a freshman in 1996, he was quite experienced as a runner. He made All-State in his first year at York.

Building Expectations

York High School cross country teams adopt the following principles:

Goals: Plan the work, work the plan.

Setbacks: Don't let runners think of themselves as a failure; despite temporary setbacks they can bounce back to greater heights than before.

Hard work: If runners really want to move up, they must be prepared to buckle down.

Persistence: A winner isn't someone who falls down the least, but the one who picks himself or herself up one more time than the competition.

Self-reliance: Always listen to the experts, we tell our runners, but we also teach them to use their own judgment, because they are the ones running the race.

Teamwork: Strong ties provide great support but also require great sacrifices.

Loyalty: Believe in the coach, teammates, oneself, and the workouts; doubt can do more to defeat a runner than any other team.

A final thought: The worth of this team isn't really measured by the events won, or the times done, or the points scored, but by whether the runners keep the values they learned and how they apply them after they leave the program.

Building Team Harmony

York cross country runners are presented with these tips and tools for team-building:

1. Get to know your teammates.
2. Go out of your way to help your teammates whenever you can.
3. Give positive feedback to your teammates whenever you get the chance.
4. Remember that both negativism and positivism are highly contagious.
5. Give 100 percent effort in practice, and work hard on your weaknesses.
6. Resolve conflicts with teammates or coaches as quickly as possible.
7. Get your attitude and disposition right *before* going to practices or meets.
8. Don't be a loudmouth or showoff.
9. Be fully responsible for yourself.
10. Be your own best igniter.
11. Communicate clearly, honestly, and openly with your coach.
12. Don't forget to have fun.

Chris Gorski embraces the 1989 team state champions.

BUILDING TEAMWORK

Once you've recruited your team, it's time to build teamwork.

1. Teamwork is the essence of life. It's how to blend the talents and strengths of individuals into a force that becomes greater than the sum of its parts.

2. Great teamwork is the only way to reach your ultimate moments, to create breakthroughs that fill your life with the sense of lasting significance.

3. Everyone is a team player, whether they know it or not. Their family, their career, their church, their neighborhood are teams.

4. Every team is a stage setting, a place to act out the drama of one's life. When runners' teams excel, they all win. Their best efforts, combined with those of their teammates, grow into something far greater and far more satisfying than anything an individual could have achieved alone. Teams make the runner a part of something that matters. They are the fountain from which all rewards will flow.

5. However, teamwork isn't simple. In fact, it can be a frustrating, elusive commodity. That's why there are so many bad teams, stuck in neutral or going downhill. Teamwork does not appear magically, just because we talk about it. It doesn't thrive just because of the presence of talent and ambition. It doesn't flourish simply because a team has tasted success.

6. Forty years of coaching has proved to me, over and over again, that the complex inner rhythms of teamwork—flows of ambition, power, cooperation, and emotion—are the keys to making dreams come true.

7. People are territorial animals. We all want to stake out something to call our own. We strike back when our turf is threatened. Don't smother those territorial and competitive instincts. They're a vital part of one's being. But harness them for the good of the team. Understand that sometimes the individual must give up some territory for the good of the team. It's an attitude: Doing one's utmost for the team will always bring something good. "Ask not what your teammates can do for you," said Magic Johnson. "Ask what you can do for your teammates."

8. The biggest reason why teams break down is they forget how they got there. In America we think "greed is good." Get all you can; who says you can't have it all? Unless we learn to manage the aftereffects of winning, the forces that lead us to the peak will turn around and destroy us. As Ben Franklin said, "Success has ruined many a man." When we begin to believe overpoweringly in our own importance we come down with the "Disease of Me."

9. The most difficult thing for an individual to do when he's part of the team is to sacrifice. It's so easy to become selfish in a team environment. Willing sacrifice is a great paradox. Runners must give up something in the immediate present—comfort, ease, recognition, hair, rewards, and so on—to attract something even better in the future: a sense that they did something that counted.

10. A team needs a covenant, an agreement that binds people together. Sometimes a covenant is written out in great detail. Sometimes it is unspoken, completely expressed through action or trust. Every team develops covenants over time, through simply being together. But some covenants are better than others, and a number of covenants are actually destructive. Flawed covenants are often built on negativity and insidious behavior. That's why there are so many bad teams out there! Any team afflicted with the "Disease of Me" functions with a tacit covenant of self-destruction.

11. Every team must decide, very consciously, to uphold covenant terms that represent the best of values: voluntary cooperation, love, hard work, and total concentration on the good of the team. The greatness flowing through the heart of the team must be pumped out to all the extremities.

12. People sometimes ask me, "What would you rather have, a winning team or a *together* team?" The answer is obvious: A team must first be together, like a big, strong family.

13. Abraham Lincoln once said, "A house divided against itself cannot stand." This is what happens when people on a team decide not to trust. Everyone will gear down their efforts until they're doing just enough to get by. Their subtle withholding of effort may eventually be enough to bring about a system-wide failure.

14. There are only two options regarding the commitment to a good covenant. Team members are *in* or they are *out*. There's no such thing in life as *in-between*.

15. Being ready isn't enough. Runners have to be *prepared*. Preparation demands mental and physical conditioning and conscious planning. A runner who is just ready and not totally prepared simply increases risk and is a liability to the team.

16. Repeated "choking" is the essence of defeatism. Losing becomes part of the runner's identity. They begin running to avoid a loss, rather than running to win. The more fearful they get, the more likely it is that their predicted disaster will ultimately come true.

17. There is a lesson that every team and every would-be winner must learn from day one: Don't back into great achievements, whether it's winning state championships or busting state records. Approach every potential great achievement in a state of total confidence.

18. When a breakthrough arrives, there will generally be some message, some voice, that captures the essence of the work to be done. It could be a movie, a novel, a song, a speech,

York J.V. women.

or a sentence rich in images. Whatever it may be, it is more than just a sign.

19. My father lay dying of lung cancer in a hospital in Miami. I flew down to see him. As I was leaving, he said to me, "Just remember what I taught you. There will come a time, and when that time comes, you go out there and kick somebody's ass." Every now and then there comes a day when someplace, some-time, we simply have to plant our feet, stand firm, and make a point about who we are and what we believe in.

20. Complacency is the last hurdle any team must overcome before attaining poten-tial greatness. Complacency is the success disease. It takes root when we're feeling good about who we are and what we've achieved after we have spent ourselves emo-tionally and physically to reach that great dream. It's so easy to accept the illusion that our struggle has ended. We've arrived, and it feels great to let go of yesterday's hunger and insecurity. From that enticing moment for-ward, it gets harder and harder to make sac-rifices. A team that has just reached a milestone is in danger. When we have momen-tum, when competitors are intimidated by our achievements, it's sometimes possible to give a half-hearted effort and still succeed. A psychology of entitlement is a looming threat. We think the top spot now belongs to us, the wins will be automatic, the rewards will never stop.

21. A classic meet-day runner is a fraud. Sloughing off in practice and workouts kills conditioning, invites injury, and ensures meet-losing fatigue. A meet-day runner is a fiction some people use to excuse themselves from working as hard as they should. Athletes who think they are meet-day runners are what coaches call "floaters." They float along on a cushion of talent or sheer speed and strength. Runners of lesser talent start beating them. Eventually every team has to learn that excel-lence isn't a destination. It's a process that must be continually improved.

22. Whoever stops being better stops be-ing good. Winners vaccinate themselves

against self-satisfaction by remembering that some rival is always planning smarter and working harder to overtake and beat a winner.

23. Excellence is never having learned enough. A few seasons in competitive sports teaches you how success can lull people. Teams that stay on top know differently—and they live it. Excellence is the gradual result of always wanting to do better. Athletes win championships through an unceasing drive to be the best. Champions will also demon-strate that hard, intelligent, relentless work is the way to winning. Excellence is the way. Mastery is the way. Challenge is the way.

24. Only by committing oneself to a tougher and constant standard of training, alertness, and performance can complacency be kept at bay. Mastery is the next goal, and mastery is built on excellence—the gradual result of al-ways wanting to do better. Mastery demands an intense awareness of the present moment and keen knowledge of one's individual best-effort potential. In getting to mastery, no mat-ter what the team or contest, precise and clearly understood information is the founda-tion. Mastery is as emotional as it is mental. Athletes can't attain mastery and neglect morale—and morale isn't simply encourage-ment. It is sparked by the will of a team's coach and its leadership to defiantly chal-lenge the team to reach for tougher new stan-dards.

25. A mission could be defined as "an im-age of a desired state that you want to get to." If that image is defined and visualized by everybody, if it is believed in, then the image will determine behavior. It will fuel motiva-tion, and it will inspire action.

26. Having a sense of mission that reaches beyond the present defines the final step to individual and team significance. That means going beyond simply being the best, going so far that you leave footprints. In our whole life, in our whole career, there may be only two or three times when we're truly on a mission of greatness. When we are, we have to know how to behave, how to perceive, and how to carry through.

The York team and fans celebrate another state championship in 1994. It was a good day.

27. At the start of a mission, two traits have to come on-line. One is courage, and the other is resolve. I like Mark Twain's definition of courage: "Courage is resistance to fear, mastery of fear—not an absence of fear." Being afraid is okay, if we are afraid with dignity. To a greater or lesser extent, fear is part of any challenge.

28. Dynasties demand determination. In sports that means we have to return to the workaday world of a new season after waging and winning war on the championship battlefield. After a glorious victory in a grand war the hardest battle to fight is the first little skirmish of the next campaign.

29. A mission is all about endurance. What runners can get for their endurance, their focus, and their hard work is the privilege of knowing that what they did really counted, really mattered. They earned that satisfaction because they committed to something bigger than themselves—a team.

30. Anteing-up means establishing an unbeatable excellence and defying others to challenge it. Instead of winning a championship, the total focus is on being a championship team, becoming historically significant and leaving footprints. Upping the ante often costs colossal exertion of effort and endurance.

31. The wisest choice a warrior can make is to sacrifice superficial self-interest and to underwrite the building of a team that supports individual skills. Warriors can only receive what they are willing to give.

32. A winner's ladder of evolution:

from NOBODY to UPSTART
from UPSTART to CONTENDER
from CONTENDER to WINNER

from WINNER to CHAMPION
from CHAMPION to DYNASTY

33. In every contest there comes a moment that distinguishes winning from losing. The true warrior understands and seizes that moment by giving an effort so intense and so intuitive that it could only be called "one from the heart." The true warrior is someone who knows how to get the job done at the moment of truth. Heart, courage, and will—these three traits define a true warrior.

34. The warrior is an immortal vision of what all winners aspire to be. That one person makes a difference to any significant team. To scale those heights demands something far stronger than the aggressive spirit to be the only person who makes a difference within a significant team. Warriors have to have love for themselves, for those who run alongside them, for the potentials inside their sport. To be a warrior, one has to be ready to give "one from the heart." For a true warrior love is more than just a sentiment. It's an attitude that leads to success.

35. Each warrior wants to leave the mark of their will, their signature, on important acts they touch. This is not the voice of ego, but of the human spirit, rising up and declaring that it has something to contribute to the solution of the hardest problems, no matter how vexing.

36. Ten simple words: The privilege of a lifetime is being who we are.

Part II

PLANNING AND TRAINING

Letter from a former York athlete to Joe Newton's team:

Many of you do not realize the magic and mystique of York cross country. You really cannot know until you are away from it and can see it from a distance, and miss it as much as I have.

When you step on the line with your green uniform on, you represent much more than a cross country team. You represent something that is as close to perfection and immortality that I have ever seen. You represent a brotherhood, a spirit, and a winning tradition that will never die.

Last year, when I got off the bus at the state meet, I believed I was one of the four luckiest guys in the world. Here I was—a 5-foot-6, 125-pound, 17-year-old kid—and I was one of four captains leading the greatest high school running dynasty in the nation.

I love York cross country. It has taught me so much and given me so many wonderful memories. I truly believe I have had teammates who will be at my wedding—and will be at my funeral. I know you will someday feel the same way I do.

Srinu Hanumadass
Class of 1995

Chapter 5

PLANNING FOR THE SEASON

Training of committed cross country runners never stops. They work year-round. With this in mind the coach must plan for the entire year, giving particular attention to the summer.

The foundation of a successful cross country season is laid before the autumn meets begin. If athletes start getting into shape when they come back to school for the fall, it's too late. They've given away too much ground to the year-round trainers. I talk in this chapter about the essential summer training. This is best done as a team but can also be an individual responsibility of runners.

Cross country season truly begins when the team comes together to train with the coach. This can range from a few weeks to several months before the meets begin. Competition starts with the new school year. You want the runners fit enough to *compete* by then. At that time your job as coach is to arrange the in-season training and meets so your athletes reach peak racing fitness for the biggest meet of the season.

Here we discuss overall seasonal patterns. Chapter 6 deals with specific workouts.

PLANNING THE YEAR

As I've said before, training must be a year-round proposition. But of course it also must vary from season to season. We work hard at York, to be sure. But it's *intelligent* hard work. We plan exactly what we want to do, and when.

Let's start with what happens at York right after the state cross country meet and go through the whole yearly cycle from there until it peaks the next fall. Most of November is down time. The runners don't rest completely, but do what we call "active rest." They might play some basketball or soccer, or they might go to the pool or the weight room. But they do little or no running for about three weeks after the state meet. This is their time to back off and regenerate.

Then in December and mid-January they build back the base that they've beaten down during the racing season. They replenish their endurance with easy-paced, unstructured running. This is winter in Illinois, you'll recall, and the runners don't usually stay outside for more than an hour.

Indoor track begins in January and blends into outdoor track, which lasts through May. Most of the runners compete in track, which I also coach. Another period of active rest follows the track season. The runners take it easy through mid-June, then start their summer buildup for cross country. We follow a structured training program.

Again I realize that you might not have the luxury of a large core group of year-round runners. Some or all of your athletes might run only in the fall and spring, while playing other sports in winter and summer. You must adjust their workouts accordingly, beginning the cross country season by consciously *undertraining* the athletes who haven't worked out all summer. Guard against breaking them down and burning them out before the season begins by using the first three or four weeks of the season as a period for getting back in shape. Focus on low mileage, little speedwork, and few if any races.

This advice also applies to first-year coaches who must play catch-up as school is about to

Coach Newton reviews the race strategy at each state meet.

start. You haven't been in contact with the runners over the summer, and they're unlikely to have done much training. Contact past members of the team to assure that they're coming back, then recruit new ones in the ways I described in chapter 4. Go into the gym classes and talk to kids face-to-face. They find it much harder to say "no" to your face than to ignore a poster on a wall or a letter in the mail.

PLANNING THE SUMMER

Some states have rules against organized workouts in the summer. But in Illinois the only restriction is that the team can't meet with the coach for the two weeks before fall practice officially begins in mid-August. The runners must run on their own during that time. I give them workout assignments, and they carry these out themselves. Our secret weapon is the captains. They make sure the other runners are doing the workouts.

In summer training we lay the groundwork for the upcoming cross country season. This is too important a period to let the training occur haphazardly. If you aren't able to work directly with your athletes during these months, at least see that each one of them has a workout schedule to follow during the summer.

Our schedule emphasizes piling up the miles. The rationale for doing this high-mileage, low-intensity training during the off-season is that it lays the endurance base for the season. Doing this work helps prevent injuries when the workouts become more intense later on. The people who get hurt tend to be those who don't do much running over the summer and start training too fast.

Putting in Miles

At York the school has summer school for both academics and athletics, and we make the summer training part of the summer-school program. Our runners pay a fee of $85 to attend for six weeks, from mid-June to the end of July. We get more attendance now that we charge than when I used to conduct this program for free as the York Track Club. They seem to perceive greater value when it costs them money.

The cross country runners come from 8 to 10 o'clock in the morning, Monday through Friday. Though the program is structured, the rules aren't as strict as they are during the fall season. We emphasize mileage. An incentive is the optional 1,000-mile club, with new members being honored with T-shirts for running that much between June 1 and September 1.

The popularity of 1,000-mile summers has waned somewhat. Some of the runners—Dan Ruecking stands out in my mind—have gone as high as 1,200 or 1,300 miles. We used to have 25 runners doing it,

and now it's down to about 10, with another 10 or 20 totaling 700 to 800 miles. We also have a 300-mile club for incoming freshmen who've signed up with the team before school starts.

PLANNING THE PRESEASON

You coaches should start official practice the very first day it's allowed in your state. This time before school starts is when you do your team-building. The first two or three weeks we're always talking about the team, bonding, empowerment, goals, and that sort of thing. This is when we decide who goes into which training group, although that changes about a half-dozen times before school starts.

The starting gun sounds, and the York sophomore team starts at the Hoffman Estates Invitational.

We get all of this done before the bulk of the freshmen join the team the first day of school. They more than double the team's size, and the practices can be a little chaotic when they first arrive. So I like to have the rest of the team running smoothly by then.

PLANNING THE EQUIPMENT

Even the most successful high school cross country programs aren't blessed with large budgets for equipment. Ours certainly isn't.

We supply the meet uniform—shorts, singlet, sweat pants, and sweat shirt. We also have jackets and rain suits available for purchase, but not everyone buys them. The runners provide their own clothing for practice, as well as their own shoes.

Shoes are the big expense. We ease this somewhat by having shoe salesmen come out to the school. They not only sell shoes at a volume discount, but give great advice on selection and fitting. I encourage the runners to buy a pair of flats and a pair of spikes. If they can only afford one, then they get the spikes.

They can train in their sneakers if they must, but this rarely happens. Other runners usually have a spare pair they can pass along. Shoes determine health and performance, and are the most important items of equipment.

Rather than get into a long discussion here about shoes, I point you to the experts. Find the best running-shoe store in your area, and ask the manager for advice on the selection and fitting of shoes for cross country. Also refer to the shoe appraisals in *Runner's World*, *Running Times*, and other magazines.

PLANNING THE DIET

You as coach can't control what your runners eat 24 hours a day. Much of this is dictated by the runner's home environment. When athletes or their parents ask about athletic nutrition, I refer them to one of the many books on this subject.

Talk to your runners about the importance of diet, especially in regard to their meals before training and competition. The prerace meal is one that a coach certainly can control when the team travels to a meet together. We don't just order off the menu, as many teams do. Instead I call ahead and tell the restaurant exactly what our runners will eat at that meal.

The proper approach to a training diet for cross country is *balance* and *moderation*. In general, mother's home cooking is the very best training table.

Runners obviously want to remain well hydrated (without becoming waterlogged), and want to avoid gaining unnecessary weight (without starving themselves). I encourage our athletes to drink 8 to 10 glasses of water a day, and not just to drink when they're thirsty. Each runner has a sports-drink bottle at workouts and races, and we take drink breaks three or four times during training.

My further recommendations deal mainly with what to do—and *not* to do—immediately before competition.

1. Avoid fried foods (they are difficult to digest), especially the day prior to and the day of a meet. At all times skip exceptionally greasy foods and any others that upset the system.

2. During the competitive season do not experiment with new foods, especially on the day of competition.

3. On meet days eat sparingly. Never eat later than four hours before competition, taking bland, nourishing foods in moderate portions.

4. Do not eat eggs on raceday, as they are composed of a sulfur base that sometimes causes gas to form, especially in a nervous stomach.

5. Before practice also watch the noon meal closely. In many ways this should be the same as the premeet meal. To be prepared for the hard afternoon training session, be especially careful not to overeat and to avoid milk at the noon meal.

The first 300 meters of the 1996 state meet. The York pack, led by Donald Sage, sticks together.

PLANNING MEDICAL CARE

Your responsibility doesn't end with requiring that each runner have a physical exam before joining the team. You also must take care of their physical complaints as the season goes along, and it's your responsibility as a coach to know basic first aid and CPR.

You need at least one doctor you can turn to quickly for medical help. This could be the parent of one of your runners, a physician who runs, or someone in the community known to treat athletes successfully.

Finding a Doctor

We have a team physician, Dr. John Durkin, who is our first line of defense against injuries. In the late 1970s I had been hearing about this podiatrist in Roselle whose brother Mike Durkin had been an Olympian twice. Next thing I knew, John was out watching a meet and we hit it off. From then on he was our medical guru.

A York runner can get in to see him immediately. We also have a number of other specialists I can call for the wide variety of problems that athletes encounter. I call this our "medical entourage" that keeps our kids ready to compete.

PLANNING THE SEASON

The first meet of the season shouldn't be rushed. Your goal should be to have the runners in top shape at the *end* of the season, for the races that count most, and not for the very first meet of the year.

The runners need a good base of training before they jump into competition. We always race for the first time on Labor Day weekend, about two weeks after the official start of practice. But this is just an intrasquad meet, and less than half of the team competes. The freshmen who didn't train in the summer sit this one out.

Our first true meet isn't until mid-September, and we wait until the end of September for our first invitational. This is really tough on us, because other schools have already run three or four of these big meets. They've gotten used to the crowd.

We have opened at the Palatine Invitational for six years in a row and have only won it twice. But in five of those years we went on to win the state meet. We like to start the season slowly and keep something in the bank for the later meets that count the most.

The temptation is to race too often. I see teams racing 18 or 20 times during the season, and feel this is too much. It doesn't leave enough time for training. We race, at most, 10 times. This includes four duals, two invitationals, the conference meet, and the state-meet series (Regional, Sectional, and State). The freshmen race only six times.

Our average for the season is less than one meet per week. This leaves us with enough training time. A runner can train 10 or 20 miles and be less tired than after racing 3 miles. The difference is in the nervous tension involved in races. By training seven or eight days when the other schools

Donald Sage winning the Downer's Grove North dual meet on September 18, 1997. He set a new course record.

are racing, we can put in an extra 50 or 100 miles during the season. That can be our winning edge at the end of the year.

To keep them fresh, some schools hold some of their best runners out of certain meets. But I don't believe in pulling anyone just because it's not a big or tough meet. This is an insult to your competition. It degrades the meet to hold out your top runners, and it's something we never do.

Planning Time Trials

At York we are constantly evaluating our cross country runners. We not only compare their times through the season, but from year to year. We have records dating back to 1960, and because the courses and distances remain consistent we can compare this year's team with those from other eras. Here is a summary of our time trials:

1. *One-mile time trial.* We run this the day before the second trial listed here. This mile gives the runners an early chance to test their speed.

2. *First intrasquad cross country meet.* We run it on our original 1.8-mile course. It's one of our most important trials, because it awards the top-12 shirts and gives these runners the choice of the best lockers.

3. *Two-man 10-mile relay.* The teams of two run alternate quarter miles on the track. This gives the top runners only about a minute's rest between laps.

4. *One-hour run.* We usually schedule this in early September, running it on our home course. It is grass, and each lap is approximately a half mile. This is a real test of stamina, and it gives us a good idea of the runners who have done their homework in the summer.

5. *Two miles on the track.* This is our run in the National Postal Competition, where times are mailed to a central office in Tucson, Arizona, for compilation.

6. *Three miles on the track.* Another postal competition, run in late October. It also gives

us a good feel for the state meet, which is the same distance.

7. *One mile on the track.* On the Monday of state meet week we time everyone at this distance. This lets the runners know if they are ready to handle the fast early pace that invariably happens at State. It's a great confidence builder.

Planning the Lineup

Deciding who makes your top seven is easy in cross country, even on a highly competitive team like ours. You have an objective standard: Who runs the fastest times on the same day and on the same course?

We base the lineup strictly on performance. Results from the most recent meet determine this meet's team. (Remember that every member of our team is competing in most of these events.) This makes every meet a challenge. Our runners compete not only to beat the other team but to maintain their position on our team.

Looking Ahead

Only the top seven get to race in the state meet. But we also take the next eight fastest underclassmen on that trip. They run a time trial on the state meet course to familiarize themselves with it for next year.

Experience means everything, so I had to figure out a way to give state meet experience on a team where the top seven were senior-oriented. The time trial on the State course is a way to acquaint the younger kids with the experience of running in that atmosphere.

PLANNING THE DETAILS

As each year progresses, I work through the following checklist of items to be taken care of before, during, and after the season.

Preseason:
1. Summer program with 1,000-mile and 300-mile shirts.
2. Preseason book.
3. Training plan for season.
4. Official practice starts in mid-August.
5. Team divided into six groups; captains appointed; shirts to top three groups.
6. Recruiting of freshmen at start of school.
7. Recruiting and assigning of managers.
8. Buying of shoes from salesman who comes to school.
9. Team one-mile, 1.8-mile, and two-man 10-mile relay time trials.
10. Alumni race on Labor Day weekend (Saturday).
11. Spiritual mission and motto for season.

In-Season:
12. Daily team meeting, roll call, name calling, checkout.
13. Standard daily workout pattern of warm-up, calisthenics, 100s, body of workout, 300, 100s, cool-down.
14. Meets approximately weekly.
15. Two time trials of two miles, one of three miles, one of one mile—all on track.
16. Team meeting after each meet; captains speak.
17. Race at state meet site one month before State; overnight trip.
18. Practice at regional meet site on Sunday before meet.
19. Practice at sectional meet site on Sunday before meet.
20. Taper begins two weeks before state meet.
21. Guest speaker in week of state meet.
22. Team awards on last day of practice; done by captains.

State Meet:
23. State champion T-shirts prepared in advance.
24. Arrangements for team travel, hotel, and meal.

25. Arrangements for band, cheerleaders, and student buses.
26. Arrangements for tuxedos and limousines.
27. Arrangements for victory celebration on return home.
28. Split-callers assigned along the course.
29. Friday workout on course.
30. Friday night team meal and movie.
31. Captains meeting with team Friday night.
32. Short run at 7:30 A.M. on raceday.
33. Team meeting at 10:30 A.M., then warm-up and the race of the year.

Postseason:

34. Limos and tuxes to awards if team wins.
35. Victory celebration on arrival home Saturday night if team wins.
36. All-school assembly on Monday; captains speak.
37. Lunch after assembly for everyone who went to state meet and all seniors.
38. Special team dinner for top seven, two weeks after State.
39. State medals for *all* who contributed to title; usually more than 50.

Andy Barrett at the 1993 state meet.

40. Team honored by School Board.
41. Team honored by City Council.
42. Visit to state capital to meet Governor, Senate, and House.
43. Awards Night; talk about each runner and show films.
44. Postseason book.

Chapter 6

PREPARING FOR PRACTICES

If you want to learn what makes a cross country team successful, don't just watch its races. What happens there is a result, not a cause. It's the end product of what these runners have done in training.

In few other sports is the ratio of training to racing greater. Each 10- to 20-minute race represents only one-tenth to one-twentieth of total running time. Cross country runners train long, hard, and often. But in few other sports is the payback for this work so dramatic on the day of competition.

Training doesn't just mean piling up mileage, though the miles do count. Training means warming up and cooling down properly, adding strength and flexibility exercises, doing race-specific speedwork, practicing the hills, and getting to know other quirks of each course. Training means knowing when to train through the small races and when to taper and peak for the big ones.

Here I talk about the workouts. They, more than any other single factor, determine your team's success.

PREPARING THE SCHEDULE

During the summer we work out in the morning, because this is when our running class is scheduled and temperatures are cooler then. After school starts, the training shifts to afternoon (except on Saturdays).

Training mileage isn't a be-all and end-all. If the miles are all slow, they only produce slow racers. But the miles do play an important part in a balanced program. We put lots of emphasis on it during the summer and in the early season. This is our base work. Then we cut down on mileage as the season progresses.

The seniors and juniors typically run between 60 and 80 miles a week; a few go up as high as 85 or 90. The sophomores run 40 to 50 miles. The freshmen peak out at only about 20 miles.

While some of these mileage figures may sound high to you, remember that the seniors and juniors have spent three or four years building to this level. Only about 10 percent of the team runs 60 or more miles a week. The majority of runners do only 40 miles or so.

Dave Walters, 11th place, has 200 meters to go in the 1996 state meet.

Training Together

At York we train together six days a week during the cross country season. The coach and the team need an occasional break from each other, and we take it on most Sundays.

Our runners are under my direct control the other six days a week. This includes every Saturday during the season, when we either have a meet or a team workout. I ask them to run on Sundays, but they're on their own then. Everyone is running at least six days, because I see to that.

The good ones train every day, and often *twice* a day. Ron Craker, one of our all-time greats, got so much out of his ability because he ran all year, ran on Sunday, ran twice a day. He won the state cross country and track two-mile championships, then went to Indiana University on a full scholarship.

PREPARING EACH DAY

The total practice session each day includes the body of the workout, a team meeting, the warm-up and cool-down, and more. This takes a fair amount of time. Our older runners come out at 2:30 in the afternoon and aren't finished until 5:00. The younger ones come at 3:30 and are done by 4:30.

As with everything else in your program, you need a daily plan. This way the runners know exactly what to expect—maybe not the details in the body of the workout but at least the overall pattern of the day. We start with a team meeting. Then comes a warm-up run of 25 to 30 minutes, followed by calisthenics (which I lead), 6 × 100-meter strides (at a fast pace), and the main workout.

We're still not finished at this point. Next comes a handicap 300-meter run in which runners start in reverse order of their abilities. This teaches them to run all-out when most tired. They follow this with another 10 × 100, then the "30-30-30" exercises (jumping jacks, push-ups, and sit-ups). Finally there's a two-mile cool-down run.

I'm a strong believer in strength and flexibility exercises. Preworkout calisthenics and the 30-30-30s are part of the daily routine. In addition, we train three times a week with weights.

Cross-training involves mixing running with other related activities such as bicycling and swimming. We don't cross-train unless we're hurt. Otherwise we just run. My theory is that a runner trains specifically for the race. A concert pianist doesn't get better by practicing on the violin but plays the piano. A runner doesn't get better by swimming but by running.

PREPARING THE WORKOUTS

Our staple workouts all involve speed. We run long, short, and medium-length intervals during the week, and segments on Saturday. (This is a less structured form of speedwork in which fast segments are run by time periods instead of distance; it is sometimes called "fartlek.") Table 6.1 shows the weekly pattern for midseason.

The Monday miles, Friday 800s, and Saturday segments are run at race pace, which improves as the season progresses. We run Tuesday's 200s at the pace that athletes plan to kick at the end of a race. Wednesday's interrupted run and Sunday's long run are at a relaxed but not-too-slow pace.

These paces, of course, vary among training groups. The less-experienced groups also scale down the volume of the workouts from those listed above for the top group.

I believe in short recovery periods between intervals. We take three minutes between the miles, two minutes between the half miles (800s), one minute between the 400s, and from a maximum of one minute to as little as 15 seconds between 200s. The rationale is that a runner doesn't get rest breaks in races and must learn to run tired.

The best place to develop a sense of pace is on the track. But runners also need to get the feel of running on the course. We're fortunate to have a state-of-the-art track. We use it for all the interval workouts.

We run on grass in the easy Wednesday workout. Our home cross country course, also grass, is the site of our Saturday segment session.

Experiencing Speed

One of my luckiest breaks in coaching was meeting Peter Coe from England, who coached his son Sebastian to a pair of Olympic gold medals and several world records. Peter spoke for Sam Bell at a track clinic at Indiana University. Sam has been my mentor for about 30 years, so I called

Table 6.1   Weekly Training Pattern

Monday	long intervals	up to 5 × 1 mile
Tuesday	short intervals	up to 4 sets of 5 × 200 meters
Wednesday	interrupted run	up to 45, 30, 30 minutes
Thursday	meet	3-mile race
Friday	midlength intervals	up to 10 × 800 meters
Saturday	segments run	up to one hour total
Sunday	individual long run	up to 15 miles

and said, "I'd love to bring Peter Coe to the clinic I have here every year." Sam put us in touch, and Peter agreed to come.

This was 1982. The next year he came back and brought Sebastian with him, and they returned in 1984 for Seb's final training before the Los Angeles Olympics.

The main thing I learned from Peter was, "You must touch on speed every day. We're training runners to race and races are fast, so you must train that way."

In this chapter I reproduce the exact workouts our top group of seven runners did at York High School during the 12 weeks of the 1996 cross country season. This program worked for us. You can use it as a guide and then make any adjustments you like to fit your particular situation. Keep in mind again that only the most experienced and mature runners on our team completed these maximum workouts. They were scaled down for the younger athletes, but the training *patterns* remain the same for all.

I just list the main part of the day's workout. Most days were preceded by a warm-up of several miles, calisthenics, and six × 100. After the main workout came a fast 300, 10 to 24 × 100, and a two-mile cool-down. A second workout of three to five miles was recommended but not required. All workouts except those on Sunday were done as a team. Briefly here's what each type of workout involves. Details appear in the 12-week schedule in Table 6.2.

- *Long.* A continuous run, usually done in Sunday workouts, apart from the team, at a comfortable pace.
- *Intervals.* These take several forms— long (miles or 1,200 meters), midlength

Warming up for the 1994 Peoria Invitational.

Table 6.2 Newton's 12 Weeks of Training

Descriptions of workout types and paces appear earlier in this chapter. Races are listed in boldface capital letters. Time trials appear in italics.

		WEEK 1
Monday	Long	23 miles in two workouts
Tuesday	Long	24 miles in two workouts
Wednesday	Intervals	25 × 400 meters, 1 minute between
Thursday	Segments	10-10-5-5-5-4-4-2 minutes
Friday	Fartlek	1 hour
Saturday	Segments	1-1-2-2-3-3-4-4-5-5-5-4-4-3-3-2-2-1 minutes
Sunday	Long	15 miles

		WEEK 2
Monday	Intervals	30 × 200 meters, 1 minute between
Tuesday	Segments	1-1-2-2-3-3-4-4-5-5-8-8-4-4-2 minutes
Wednesday	Intervals	10 × 800 meters, 2 minutes between
Thursday	Run	30 minutes cross country
Friday	*Time Trial*	*1 mile track, 10-minute recovery*
	Intervals	10 × 400 meters, 10 × 200 meters; 1 minute between
Saturday	*Time Trial*	*1.8 miles cross country, 15-minute recovery*
	Interval	8 minutes fast
Sunday	Long	15 miles

		WEEK 3
Monday	*Time Trial*	*2-man 10-mile track relay (20 × 400 meters, about 1 minute between)*
Tuesday	Killer Dillers	30 minutes of sprint 50 meters, jog 60
Wednesday	Intervals	30 × 200 meters, 1 minute between
Thursday	Interrupted	45-30-30 minutes
Friday	Intervals	7 × 1,200 meters, 4 minutes between
Saturday	Segments	1-1-2-2-3-3-4-6-6-6-4-4-2-2-2-2-2-1 minutes
Sunday	Long	15 miles

		WEEK 4
Monday	Interrupted	45-45-30 minutes
Tuesday	Interrupted	45-45-30 minutes
Wednesday	Intervals	25 × 400 meters
Thursday	Segments	10-10-5-5-5-4-4-2 minutes
Friday	Fartlek	1 hour
Saturday	*Time Trial*	*1-hour cross country run for distance*
Sunday	Long	15 miles

(continued)

continued

Week 5		
Monday	Intervals	5 × 1 mile, 3 minutes between
Tuesday	Intervals	4 sets of 5 × 200 meters, 60 seconds between in first set, then 45, 30, 15
Wednesday	Interrupted	45-30-30 minutes
THURSDAY	**RACE**	**DUAL MEET**
Friday	Intervals	10 × 800 meters, 2 minutes between
Saturday	Segments	1-1-2-2-2-2-4-4-6-6-6-4-4-2-2-2-2-1 minutes
Sunday	Long	15 miles

Week 6		
Monday	Intervals	20 × 400 meters, 1 minute between
Tuesday	Intervals	4 sets of 5 × 200 meters, 60 seconds between in first set, then 45, 30, 15
Wednesday	Interrupted	45-30-30 minutes
THURSDAY	**RACE**	**DUAL MEET**
Friday	Prerace	6 × 200 meters, jog back to start
SATURDAY	**RACE**	**INVITATIONAL MEET**

Week 7		
Monday	Intervals	3 × 1 mile, 3 minutes between
Tuesday	Intervals	4 sets of 5 × 200 meters, 60 seconds between in first set, then 45, 30, 15
Wednesday	Interrupted	45-30-30 minutes
THURSDAY	**RACE**	**DUAL MEET**
Friday	Prerace	6 × 200 meters, jog back to start
SATURDAY	**RACE**	**INVITATIONAL MEET**
Sunday	Long	15 miles

Week 8		
Monday	Intervals	4 × 1 mile, 3 minutes between
Tuesday	Intervals	4 sets of 5 × 200 meters, 60 seconds between in first set, then 45, 30, 15
Wednesday	Interrupted	45-30-30 minutes
THURSDAY	**RACE**	**DUAL MEET**
Friday	Intervals	12 × 800 meters, 2 minutes between
Saturday	Segments	8-8-6-6-6-3-3-3-3-2-2-2-2-1 minutes
Sunday	Long	15 miles

continued

Week 9		
Monday	*Time Trial*	*2 miles track, 15-minute recovery*
	Intervals	2 × 1 mile, 3 minutes between
Wednesday	Interrupted	45-30-30 minutes
Thursday	Intervals	3 × 400 meters very fast, 3 minutes between
Friday	Prerace	6 × 200 meters, jog back to start
SATURDAY	**RACE**	**CONFERENCE MEET**
Sunday	Prerace	4 × 400 on regional meet course, jog back to start

Week 10		
Monday	*Time Trial*	*3 miles track, 15-minute recovery*
	Interval	1 mile fast
Tuesday	Intervals	4 sets of 5 × 200 meters, 60 seconds between in first set, then 45-30-15
Wednesday	Interrupted	45-30-15 minutes
Thursday	Intervals	3 × 400 meters very fast, 3 minutes between
Friday	Prerace	6 × 200 meters, jog back to start
SATURDAY	**RACE**	**REGIONAL MEET**
Sunday	Prerace	4 × 400 on sectional meet course, jog back to start

Week 11		
Monday	*Time Trial*	*2 miles track, 15-minute recovery*
	Interval	1 mile fast
Tuesday	Intervals	4 sets of 5 × 200 meters, 60 seconds between in first set, then 45, 30, 15
Wednesday	Interrupted	45-30-15 minutes
Thursday	Intervals	3 × 400 meters very fast, 3 minutes between
Friday	Prerace	6 × 200 meters
SATURDAY	**RACE**	**SECTIONAL MEET**
Sunday	Long	12 miles

Week 12		
Monday	*Time Trial*	*1 mile track, 10-minute recovery*
	Interval	1 mile fast
Tuesday	Intervals	2 sets of 5 × 200 meters, 45 seconds between in first set, then 15
Wednesday	Interrupted	45-30-15 minutes
Thursday	Intervals	3 × 400 meters very fast, 3 minutes between
Friday	Prerace	6 × 200 on state meet course, jog back to start
SATURDAY	**RACE**	**STATE MEET (end of season)**

(800 meters), and short (400s or 200s). We emphasize short recovery periods (listed with each interval workout below).

- *Segments.* We run these on the cross country course, with the fast segment being a time period with a whistle signaling the start and end of each. The recovery period is always one minute.

- *Fartlek.* This is the Swedish word for "speed play," an unstructured mixture of faster and easier running.

- *Time Trial* (italicized in the schedule). It's much like a race but involves only our own team.

Marius Bakken, York's best distance runner ever, showing an outstanding finishing kick at the end of the 1995 Peoria Invitational.

- *Killer Dillers.* This workout, adopted from renowned coach Arthur Lydiard, alternates 50-meter sprints and 60-meter jogs for an extended time.

- *Interrupted.* We take five-minute breaks a couple of times during our team long runs. No extra warm-up or cool-down mileage on these days.

- *Prerace.* An easy workout, usually taken the day before a meet.

- *Race* (capitalized boldface in the schedule). Actual competition. We raced 10 times in 1996.

PREPARING FOR MEETS

You prepare your runners for the courses on which they'll race. Most of ours, including the state meet course, happen to be flat. While hill training isn't a great concern to us, we do travel to practice on hills a half-dozen times during the summer. If our biggest meets were hilly, we'd also have to seek out something comparable in the fall because we don't have any hills near our school.

Experience on the actual course of an upcoming meet is vital. You don't want your runners to get acquainted with it for the first time on raceday. We train the regional and sectional meet courses ahead of time. We always run the state meet course a month before at an invitational, and we train again on that course the day before State.

Your runners can't focus equal attention on every meet. It would take too much time away from training to be resting before and after each one. We train right through all but the last two meets of the season. The only ones we taper for are the Sectional and State.

The week of the Sectional our training drops about 30 percent below normal. It falls radically, by about 50 percent, the week of State. This ensures that everyone will be fresh and rarin' to go on The Day.

1997 Palatine Invitational champions. The York team placed first of 22 teams with 39 points. From left to right: Collin Lawrence, Tom Moore, Donald Sage, Noah Lawrence, Paul Launius, David Genovese, and Jim Mallaney.

Part III

TEACHING TECHNIQUES AND TACTICS

Letter from a former York athlete to Joe Newton:

When I entered your cross country program in June 1992, I was completely oblivious to what I was getting into. What you have done for me in four years is incredible. Thank you for helping me become a leader. You took a risk by making me, someone who is not the number one runner, the team captain.

I always wanted to run in the state meet, but instead I will have to settle for running my personal best. It is that personal record that matters most, not trophies or medals. When I look back at my high school years, what I'll remember most will be your friendship, love, and commitment to excellence.

James Sheridan
Class of 1996

Chapter 7

TEACHING PROPER RUNNING FORM

Cross country is elegantly simple in style. Get from Point A to Point Z as fast as possible. No prizes are awarded for looking good. If they were, Emil Zatopek never would have won anything. Zatopek wore a seriously pained expression and used a high-shouldered, thrashing arm action. Yet no one but him has ever won the 5,000, 10,000, and marathon in the same Olympics.

A runner's basic form is imprinted at birth and in the years before reaching your team. That said, however, the form isn't as indelible as a fingerprint. Certain energy-wasting form flaws can be ironed out. And certain specialized types of running form, such as going up and down hills or launching into a finishing kick, can and should be taught. This chapter tells you what can be changed and what should be left alone.

TEACHING IDEAL FORM

Good running form for cross country is good form, *period*. It applies to all types of distance running—over the country, on the track, or on the road. Much of my advice comes from the great University of Oregon coach, Bill Bowerman. His term was, "Run tall."

York women running at a 1995 dual meet.

Run upright, in other words, with the hips thrust slightly forward. Don't lean forward or backward, but keep the body over the feet. This keeps the runner balanced, which is especially important on the varied and sometimes rough terrain of cross country. When the torso is over the feet, overstriding isn't possible. Bowerman advised keeping the head balanced on the shoulders. Look straight ahead, not down at the feet or up at the sky.

We also emphasize arm action. Draw an imaginary line down the middle of the chest.

Don't let the hands swing across this line, or an inefficient twisting motion in the body will result. The arm action forward and backward should be an arc in which the elbow doesn't pass in front of the hip on the upswing, and the hand doesn't go behind the hip on the backswing. The hands are held lightly cupped, neither tightly clenched nor open, with the thumb resting on the forefinger.

In summary, these are the basics of running form that we teach:

1. *Head position.* Look straight ahead at the course, not up or down. This will keep the chin down and neck relaxed. When fatigue sets in, many runners throw their head back. Not only does it cause tension and alter the body angle, but it also makes it much harder to breathe just when more oxygen is needed (see figure 7.1).

Figure 7.1 Head position.

2. *Body angle.* Run tall. Keep the body balanced over the legs, as if an imaginary plumb line could be dropped from the head right down to the feet. While running uphill, lean

forward into the hill, but lean with the whole body and not just bending from the waist. Running downhill, keep the body angle perpendicular to the ground; this requires leaning forward again with the entire body (see figure 7.1).

3. *Arm action.* Carry the arms in a low-medium position, never high on the chest. This means the arms will be almost at right angles. Use a natural swing forward and backward, with the hand not going above shoulder level on the forward swing or behind the seam of the shorts on the backswing. Never let the hands pass the center line of the chest. Swing the arms from the shoulder (think of a pin driven through the shoulders from which all swing originates). The shoulders should not move, at least noticeably, from a right angle to the ground. Sway of the shoulders will cut speed (see figure 7.2).

Figure 7.2 Arm action.

4. *Elbows.* Keep them three to five inches away from the sides of the body. Above all else make sure the elbows stay unlocked, ranging from about a 90-degree angle as the arm moves forward to a 135-degree angle as it

comes backward. Locked elbows result in shoulder sway.

5. *Hands.* Keep the hands relaxed and the wrists loose. Cup the hands and touch the thumb to the forefinger.

6. *Knee action.* Let the leg come forward with as little effort as possible, which means low knee lift. The leg acts as a pendulum, and its weight carries it forward.

7. *Footplant.* Land on the lower part of the ball of the foot, drop the heel, and push off the ball of the foot. Do not let the heel "slap" or hit first, and do not turn your feet out. Tell them to listen to themselves when they run; they should hear nothing (see figure 7.3).

8. *Stride length.* Don't overstride; this is a cardinal sin of running. Avoid reaching for the next stride. If you concentrate on "running

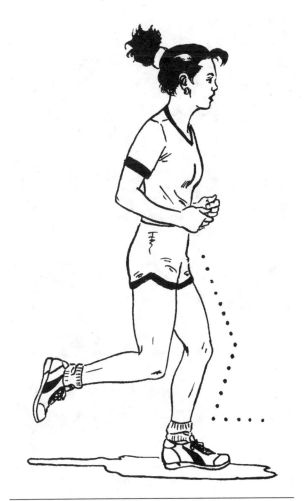

Figure 7.3 Footplant.

tall" with a low forward knee lift, overstriding should not be a problem. A rule of thumb: the longer the distance, the shorter the stride.

9. *Breathing.* Keep three important points in mind: (a) breathe deeply, (b) breathe regularly, and (c) inhale and exhale through the nose and mouth together.

10. *Relaxation.* Avoid unnecessary use of energy through tension and stress originating in the face, particularly in the lower jaw. Let the lower jaw be so relaxed that it will actually give the appearance of flopping around. This will also give runners the appearance of smiling, which will work wonders when they pass an opponent at a crucial point in the race. Another sign of tension appears in the hands and then the arms. Keep the hands relaxed. If the arms tire, drop and shake them occasionally to promote circulation.

It was a gamble to put sophomore Tom Moore into the 1996 state meet, but it paid off. He rose to become our fourth man.

TEACHING INDIVIDUAL FORM

It's valuable for runners to have a mental picture of what ideal running form is. But there's no need to harp on it all the time. We see some runners who are poetry in motion and others whose form can only be described as ragged. Yet they can achieve equally good results.

Looking Okay

When speaking of running form, a York runner named Don DeMent comes to mind. I called him "Hollywood" because he wore dark glasses. He was just a little guy, 5-6 and 115 pounds, with form that wasn't pretty to watch. He ran slew-footed, like a duck, with elbows in and hands out.

Hollywood looked very awkward, but he had a heart that was unbelievable. He led our team to the state championship in 1965 by placing fifth. I didn't fool with his form—never even mentioned it to him. If a runner is doing okay, why bother him?

I've noticed that the new freshman runners tend to have the most problems. Most of these iron themselves out naturally as the runners train, get stronger, and improve their running efficiency.

TEACHING PROBLEM CORRECTION

Major form problems often have to do with mistaken ideas of what distance-running form is. Athletes may come in thinking they have to run on their toes like the sprinters they see on television. Or they imagine that the longer their stride is, the faster they'll go.

Their mental images are 180 degrees off. Distance runners land on the ball of the foot, drop to the heel, and then push off the ball. And an overly long stride is inefficient. The longer the race is, the shorter the stride.

These are both correctable defects. So are the problems with body lean and arm action described earlier. Generally, though, I work within the fairly wide boundaries of what is okay, calling attention to flaws only when absolutely necessary. We don't want to take attention away from training by harping on form all the time.

During a workout it's better not to shout at runners about problems with their form. This embarrasses them in front of their teammates. Instead, take the runner aside and say, "I've been watching you and . . ." Kids want to be coached. They respond if you make corrections in a constructive way. If what you say is correct, they'll get an immediate payback in faster times.

Correcting Quietly

Let me share a personal story about pointing out problems with form. I went through my high school years with no one ever commenting on my form. When I got to Northwestern, Coach Rut Walter pointed out my lousy arm action. They swung across the midline of my body and caused me to do the twist.

The advice eventually helped me improve, but at the time it was embarrassing to be told that I'd been running wrong all those years. I try to remember this and correct our runners by pointing out their errors quickly and quietly.

TEACHING RELAXATION

Tension is a tricky matter, because before a race it is normal—maybe even *essential*—to feel tense. This gets the competitive juices flowing. But excessive tension shouldn't carry over into the race, or even the workout. A tense athlete is running with the brakes on, while relaxed form lets the power come out.

You can read more about the mental aspects of prerace tension in chapter 10; here we deal mainly with the physical. Tension begins in the arms and the jaw, and can be released there. We shout out to tight runners, "Drop your arms; shake 'em out . . . Let your jaw hang loose . . . Stay smooth."

TEACHING CROSS COUNTRY FORM

On rough surfaces, don't worry so much about form as about not hurting anyone. On a rugged course, the runner's first concern is protecting himself from stepping in a pothole or rut, or slipping while running across concrete in spiked shoes.

We always practice on the course before racing there. This includes workouts on the courses where major races are run, plus a warming up there on raceday. During these sessions we memorize the course conditions, remembering the location of the hills, the ruts, the soft or muddy spots, the sidewalks, the narrow areas that might cause trouble.

Every cross country course is different, and it can even differ from day to day depending on weather. Runners need to "read" it before they race it.

TEACHING HILL RUNNING

Pay the most attention to the placement and size of hills on the course. Many runners have an exaggerated fear of hills. They should realize that skilled climbers can enjoy a great tactical advantage here.

I tell my runners, when coming to a hill be ready to move. Attack the hill. Try to pass people on the way up. Lean forward, shorten the stride, drive more with the knees, pump harder with the arms. If they do all this, they're guaranteed to pass people who are just slogging up the hill, wondering when it's going to end.

For downhill running the old theory was lean back and let gravity take over. Fly down the hill, trying to make up the ground lost on the way up. This took a big toll in pounding as runners banged down on their heels. The new theory is to lean slightly forward, keeping the body perpendicular to the slope. Runners still go fast this way but maintain some control instead of racing wildly downhill. I like the new theory: Go smoothly down the hill.

TEACHING BREATHING

Arthur Lydiard was asked this question: "Should I breathe through my nose or mouth?" His answer: "You breathe through your nose and your mouth, and your eyes and ears if that were possible. Get the air in any way you can."

Breathing is obviously important. Runners need gallons of oxygen, and they'll get it by just breathing. They don't need to worry about

counting breaths or timing them with their footsteps. Tell them to focus on their running, and the breathing will take care of itself.

TEACHING PACE CHANGING

The pace varies widely during the race: fast (often too fast) at the start, slower uphill, faster downhill, very fast (you hope) at the end. So you must train your runners to handle *any* pace. We train at a wide range of paces, as you noticed in chapter 6.

We practice shifting gears by running a set of 100-meter sprints at the end of our workouts. We also do it in some of the segment work, when I blow a whistle with 15 seconds to go and the runners shift gears. This simulates kicking at the end of the race: getting up more on the toes, lifting the knees higher, pumping the arms harder. Runners may think they're tired at this point, but shifting gears allows them to recruit fresher muscles and tap new reserves.

Bob Reed kicks his way through the crowd in the 1989 state meet.

Shifting Gears

I saw the value of shifting gears when Sebastian Coe trained with us before the 1984 Olympics. He was here 12 days, and I had my kids out watching everything that he did. Seb's visit here had a profound effect on the program for years to come.

He would place a cone at the 70-meter mark of his 100-meter sprints. Seb already seemed to be sprinting, then—bang!—he would find an even higher gear when he reached the cone. That summer his kick helped him win the Olympic 1,500-meter gold medal and set the still-standing Olympic record.

Chapter 8

IMPROVING RUNNERS' PERFORMANCE

Just as no style points are awarded in cross country, neither does anyone win anything by being first after the opening quarter mile of a race. Yet you could hardly tell it by watching the start of high school meets.

Runners who are long on enthusiasm and short on experience start like quarter horses, bolting off the line as if the race ended less than a minute later. Then as the race wears on their pace winds down, only to revive briefly during a final spurt. The fact that most races are run this way doesn't make it right. Better racing results from more even pacing.

Pace. That's the essential skill taught in this chapter. You want your runners to know how to spread their energy smoothly over the entire distance. You want them to develop a clock in their head by practicing pacing on the track. You want them to run strongly all the way, and to be up front at the end where the prizes *are* awarded.

Split callers at the three-quarter mile 1995 Palatine Invitational. Ryan Bredemeyer of York leading.

Pacing Properly

We got the supreme compliment of all time in the 1960s. A sports editor named Karl Schindl of the *Elmhurst Press* wrote, "York's runners took two steps and were right on pace."

Our athletes do indeed have a pacing plan for every race. They definitely do *not* try to go out fast. The race is not won there but can be *lost* there. The race is won at the end, and we want to be in the hunt when it counts instead of falling victim to a crazy early pace that kills off the runners who attempt it.

Some young athletes need convincing that this is the proper approach. I tell them, "Look at the record. We have 19 state titles. We've won more than 200 conference championships. The proof is in the pud-

ding." If they start too fast, they're going to be in agony long before the race is over. Is that any way to feel?

IMPROVING RACE PACING

The best way to run a race, in pacing terms, is cautiously at the start, strong in the middle, hard at the end. That's our standard practice.

Even pace might theoretically be the best way to run a race, but it never works out to be perfectly even. It might work on the track, but is not practical when dealing with the uneven terrain of cross country. Every course is different, and runners need to take that into account in the pacing plan. The pace varies, but within a fairly narrow range.

A runner certainly shouldn't do the first mile in five minutes, the other miles in six or seven minutes. That's too big a variation on any course and shows that the pacing plan needs some serious adjusting.

"Negative splits" is another good way to pace a race. This means running the second half of the race in less time than the first. The difference is a negative number—but a positive experience.

I love negative splits and encourage our runners to try for them. This might work out, for our very best runners, to a 5:00 first mile, 4:55 second, and 4:50 third. They'll often go five or more seconds slower for the first mile than the second. This is more a matter of working their way through traffic than intentionally holding back. We do hold back at the start, but not too much.

IMPROVING PACE JUDGMENT

Runners learn pace by practicing it, and the best place to do that pacework is on the track. We do all our interval training and most of our time trials on the track. We know that track measurements are accurate (cross country courses often aren't). Conditions are also constant on the track, and we can compare interval times from week to week.

A different runner leads each of the intervals. That way everybody gets the feeling of setting the pace. They get pretty good at pacing after awhile. They come within a few tenths of a second of the target time for a 200 or 400, having developed that "clock in the head" that we want.

We don't even bother checking the pace when running segment workouts on the cross country course. The runners know how fast they're going by then from the homework they have done on the track.

IMPROVING PACE PLANS

We use a chart with the runners' names on it. We have one chart each for the varsity, sophomores, and freshmen. We've measured each

Melissa Mack and Mary Beth Driscoll, 1986.

course we run and noted where every quarter mile is. The chart lists target quarter times for each course and for each runner.

Our computer person helps put this together. It's a lot of work, but it pays off in the end. The York runners don't concern themselves too much with beating another runner. They concentrate on following the plan.

The ideal is to call everyone's split time at each quarter. But this isn't always possible, or even allowed at some meets. We station someone at every quarter-mile point at most meets to shout out times. However, no one can do this at State except the officials, who give times only at the half mile, mile, and two miles.

Our managers still stand at the quarters to record times silently. We review them later to see how everyone's pace stacked up—here's where they picked up, here's where they let down. The older runners have already figured it out for themselves.

In addition we take a distance-measuring clicker to the state meet. The day of the race, we walk back from the finish line and note landmarks for 150, 220, 330, 440, and 660 yards to go. Observers think we don't trust the course distance and are remeasuring it. But we're just checking where to do our gear-shifting as the end nears.

IMPROVING MIDRACE PACE

As discussed, most high school races start at breakneck speed—too fast in my opinion. This leads to slowing down too much in midrace. Races are won in the middle. The jackrabbit starters turn to tortoises then, slowing down radically.

We run the middle mile hard, running the heck out of it, passing the runners who are dragging. With a mile to go, we try to be poised to win. Then we hang on in the last mile and kick with reckless abandon at the end.

IMPROVING FINISHING KICK

Here's where the concept of gears (discussed in chapter 7) really comes into play. A well-prepared runner who has run a smart pace can shift gears several times in the home-stretch.

Our runners start to accelerate with a quarter to go. The big kick begins 300 meters out, which is why we practice 300s all season at the end of the workout when they're tired. They have done this dozens of times in training, so it's no problem now. About 150 yards out they try to find yet another gear. I tell them, "Nobody passes you in that last 150. Run with reckless abandon."

The greatest thing in life is not in never having fallen, but in rising up again. Jim Beck, 1995.

Newton's Pace Chart

We assign each runner splits to aim for at each of the checkpoints. This is labeled "Pace" on the following chart (figure 8.1). Actual splits are recorded in the "Race" boxes. See also the pace tables in figures 8.2 and 8.3.

Pace Chart

At Peoria

Meet _State Meet Time Trial_   **Date** _Friday, November 8, 1996_

Weather _Cloudy 50°_

Mr. Newton   Marinier
M. Cioni
Twin #1

Time Trial

		(220)	440	880	3/4	(Mile)	1 1/4	1 1/2	(1 3/4)	2	2 1/4	(2 1/2)	Chute	3
Mallaney	Race	32	72	2:32	4:09	5:21	6:55	8:17	9:52	11:11	12:45	14:06	15:29	16:52
	Pace	36	73	2:33	3:52	5:11	6:30	7:54	9:21	10:10	12:05	13:21	14:29	15:45
P. Cioni	Race	32	72	2:33	4:09	5:23	6:54	8:11	9:44	11:06	12:34	13:57	15:13	16:32
	Pace	37	74	2:35	3:56	5:16	6:36	8:01	9:30	10:50	12:16	13:34	14:43	16:00
Marinier	Race	32	72	2:33	4:09	5:20	6:47	8:05	9:34	10:52	12:21	13:42	15:01	16:23
	Pace	38	76	2:38	4:00	5:21	6:43	8:09	9:39	11:01	12:28	13:46	14:57	16:15
Twin #1	Race	32	73	2:32	4:09	5:20	6:47	8:05	9:35	10:51	12:17	13:35	14:50	16:09
	Pace	38	76	2:38	4:00	5:21	6:43	8:09	9:39	11:01	12:28	13:46	14:57	16:15
Launius	Race	32	73	2:34	4:09	5:23	6:54	8:11	9:45	11:06	12:36	13:58	15:18	16:40
	Pace	40	80	2:40	4:04	5:26	6:49	8:16	9:48	11:11	12:39	13:59	15:11	16:30
Bredemeyer	Race	32	74	2:35	4:09	5:30	7:00	8:20	9:54	11:12	12:43	14:02	15:16	16:34
	Pace	41	82	2:42	4:08	5:31	6:55	8:23	9:57	11:21	12:50	14:12	15:25	16:45
Pebble	Race	32	74	2:36	4:12	5:35	7:04	8:28	10:05	11:29	13:09	14:33	16:00	17:26
	Pace	41	82	2:42	4:08	5:31	6:55	8:23	9:57	11:21	12:50	14:12	15:25	16:45
Thomas	Race	32	73	2:35	4:12	5:24	6:57	8:19	9:54	11:12	12:40	14:00	15:19	16:33
	Pace	42	85	2:48	4:12	5:37	7:01	8:30	10:06	11:31	13:01	14:25	15:39	17:00
	Race													
	Pace													
	Race													
	Pace													
	Race													
	Pace													
	Race													
	Pace													

Figure 8.1 Pace chart.

Newton's Two-Mile (3,000-Meter) Pace Table

Given the choice, I would prefer even pace for all distances. However, after studying hundreds of races I've seen that this is not often practical. Two-mile and 3,000-meter races are usually run with the first and last quarter miles slightly faster than the overall average pace. We base the pace table below on this fact. Note that the pace is negative, with the second mile being run a little faster than the first. Select a time goal from the left-hand column, then note the corresponding splits. Some states run 3,000-meter (3K) races, so equivalent times are listed for that distance in the second column. This table presumes a flat course, so make time adjustments for hills.

2 mi	3K	1/4	1/2	3/4	mi	1 1/4	1 1/2	1 3/4
9:00	8:23	1:06	2:15	3:23	4:31	5:38	6:47	7:55
9:10	8:33	1:08	2:17	3:27	4:36	5:44	6:54	8:03
9:20	8:42	1:09	2:20	3:31	4:41	5:51	7:02	8:12
9:30	8:52	1:10	2:22	3:34	4:46	5:57	7:09	8:21
9:40	9:01	1:11	2:25	3:38	4:51	6:03	7:17	8:30
9:50	9:10	1:13	2:27	3:42	4:56	6:09	7:24	8:35
10:00	9:19	1:14	2:30	3:46	5:01	6:16	7:32	8:47
10:10	9:29	1:15	2:32	3:49	5:06	6:22	7:39	8:56
10:20	9:38	1:16	2:35	3:53	5:11	6:28	7:47	9:05
10:30	9:48	1:18	2:37	3:57	5:16	6:34	7:54	9:13
10:40	9:57	1:19	2:40	4:01	5:21	6:41	8:02	9:22
10:50	10:06	1:20	2:42	4:04	5:26	6:47	8:09	9:31
11:00	10:15	1:21	2:45	4:08	5:31	6:53	8:17	9:40
11:10	10:25	1:23	2:47	4:12	5:36	6:59	8:24	9:48
11:20	10:34	1:24	2:50	4:16	5:41	7:06	8:32	9:57
11:30	10:44	1:25	2:52	4:19	5:46	7:12	8:39	10:06
11:40	10:53	1:26	2:55	4:23	5:51	7:18	8:47	10:15
11:50	11:02	1:28	2:57	4:27	5:56	7:24	8:54	10:23
12:00	11:11	1:29	3:00	4:31	6:01	7:31	9:02	10:32
12:10	11:21	1:30	3:02	4:34	6:06	7:37	9:09	10:41
12:20	11:30	1:31	3:05	4:38	6:11	7:43	9:17	10:50
12:30	11:40	1:33	3:07	4:42	6:16	7:49	9:24	10:58
12:40	11:49	1:34	3:10	4:46	6:21	7:56	9:32	11:07
12:50	11:58	1:35	3:12	4:49	6:26	8:02	9:39	11:16
13:00	12:07	1:36	3:15	4:53	6:31	8:08	9:47	11:25
13:10	12:17	1:38	3:17	4:57	6:36	8:14	9:54	11:33
13:20	12:26	1:39	3:20	5:01	6:41	8:21	10:02	11:42
13:30	12:36	1:40	3:22	5:04	6:46	8:27	10:09	11:51
13:40	12:45	1:41	3:25	5:08	6:51	8:33	10:17	12:00
13:50	12:54	1:43	3:27	5:12	6:56	8:39	10:25	12:08
14:00	13:03	1:44	3:30	5:16	7:01	8:46	10:32	12:17
14:10	13:13	1:45	3:32	5:19	7:06	8:52	10:39	12:26
14:20	13:22	1:46	3:35	5:23	7:11	8:58	10:47	12:35
14:30	13:32	1:48	3:37	5:27	7:16	9:04	10:54	12:43
14:40	13:41	1:49	3:40	5:31	7:21	9:11	11:02	12:52
14:50	13:50	1:50	3:42	5:34	7:26	9:17	11:09	13:01

Figure 8.2 Two-mile pace table.

Newton's Three-Mile (5,000-Meter) Pace Table

Some states run three miles, others 5,000 meters (5K). We list target times for these distances in the first two columns, then the pace breakdowns. They are not perfectly even, allowing slightly faster running at the start and finish. However, the second 1 1/2 miles is a little faster than the first, giving a negative split. The times are based on flat courses and may need adjusting for hills. Select a time goal on the left, then find the appropriate quarter-mile splits across the page.

3 mi	5K	1/4	1/2	3/4	mi	1 1/4	1 1/2	1 3/4	2 mi	2 1/4	2 1/2	2 3/4
14:00	14:30	1:09	2:19	3:30	4:40	5:50	7:03	8:15	9:27	10:34	11:43	12:51
14:10	14:40	1:09	2:21	3:32	4:43	5:55	7:08	8:21	9:33	10:41	11:51	13:00
14:20	14:50	1:10	2:23	3:35	4:46	5:59	7:13	8:26	9:40	10:49	11:59	13:10
14:30	15:01	1:11	2:24	3:37	4:50	6:03	7:18	8:32	9:47	10:56	12:08	13:19
14:40	15:11	1:12	2:26	3:40	4:53	6:07	7:23	8:38	9:53	11:04	12:16	13:28
14:50	15:21	1:13	2:28	3:42	4:56	6:11	7:28	8:44	10:00	11:11	12:24	13:37
15:00	15:32	1:14	2:29	3:45	5:00	6:15	7:33	8:50	10:07	11:19	12:33	13:46
15:10	15:42	1:14	2:31	3:47	5:03	6:20	7:38	8:56	10:13	11:26	12:41	13:55
15:20	15:52	1:15	2:33	3:50	5:06	6:24	7:43	9:01	10:20	11:34	12:49	14:05
15:30	16:02	1:16	2:34	3:52	5:10	6:28	7:48	9:07	10:27	11:41	12:58	14:14
15:40	16:13	1:17	2:36	3:55	5:13	6:32	7:53	9:13	10:33	11:49	13:06	14:23
15:50	16:24	1:18	2:38	3:57	5:16	6:36	7:58	9:19	10:40	11:56	13:14	14:32
16:00	16:35	1:19	2:39	4:00	5:20	6:40	8:03	9:25	10:47	12:04	13:23	14:41
16:10	16:45	1:19	2:41	4:02	5:23	6:45	8:08	9:31	10:53	12:11	13:31	14:50
16:20	16:55	1:20	2:43	4:05	5:26	6:49	8:13	9:36	11:00	12:19	13:39	15:00
16:30	17:06	1:21	2:44	4:07	5:30	6:53	8:18	9:42	11:07	12:26	13:48	15:09
16:40	17:16	1:22	2:46	4:10	5:33	6:57	8:23	9:48	11:13	12:34	13:56	15:18
16:50	17:26	1:23	2:48	4:12	5:36	7:01	8:28	9:54	11:20	12:41	14:04	15:27
17:00	17:37	1:24	2:49	4:15	5:40	7:05	8:33	10:00	11:27	12:49	14:13	15:36
17:10	17:47	1:24	2:51	4:17	5:43	7:10	8:38	10:06	11:33	12:56	14:21	15:45
17:20	17:57	1:25	2:53	4:20	5:46	7:14	8:43	10:11	11:40	13:04	14:29	15:55
17:30	18:08	1:26	2:54	4:22	5:50	7:18	8:48	10:17	11:47	13:11	14:38	16:04
17:40	18:18	1:27	2:56	4:25	5:53	7:22	8:53	10:23	11:53	13:19	14:46	16:13
17:50	18:28	1:28	2:58	4:27	5:56	7:26	8:58	10:29	12:00	13:26	14:54	16:22
18:00	18:39	1:29	2:59	4:30	6:00	7:30	9:03	10:35	12:07	13:34	15:03	16:31
18:10	18:49	1:29	3:01	4:32	6:03	7:35	9:08	10:41	12:13	13:41	15:11	16:40
18:20	18:59	1:30	3:03	4:35	6:06	7:39	9:13	10:46	12:20	13:49	15:19	16:50
18:30	19:10	1:31	3:04	4:37	6:10	7:43	9:18	10:52	12:27	13:56	15:28	16:59
18:40	19:20	1:32	3:06	4:40	6:13	7:47	9:23	10:58	12:33	14:04	15:36	17:08
18:50	19:30	1:33	3:08	4:42	6:16	7:51	9:28	11:04	12:40	14:11	15:44	17:17
19:00	19:41	1:34	3:09	4:45	6:20	7:55	9:33	11:10	12:47	14:19	15:53	17:26
19:10	19:51	1:34	3:11	4:47	6:23	8:00	9:38	11:16	12:53	14:26	16:01	17:35
19:20	20:01	1:35	3:13	4:50	6:26	8:04	9:43	11:21	13:00	14:34	16:09	17:45
19:30	20:12	1:36	3:14	4:52	6:30	8:08	9:48	11:27	13:07	14:41	16:18	17:54
19:40	20:22	1:37	3:16	4:55	6:33	8:12	9:53	11:33	13:13	14:49	16:26	18:03
19:50	20:32	1:38	3:18	4:57	6:36	8:16	9:58	11:39	13:20	14:56	16:34	18:12
20:00	20:43	1:39	3:19	5:00	6:40	8:20	10:03	11:45	13:27	15:04	16:43	18:21
20:10	20:53	1:39	3:21	5:02	6:43	8:25	10:08	11:51	13:33	15:11	16:51	18:30
20:20	21:04	1:40	3:23	5:05	6:46	8:29	10:13	11:56	13:40	15:19	16:59	18:40
20:30	21:14	1:41	3:24	5:07	6:50	8:33	10:18	12:02	13:47	15:26	17:08	18:49

(continued)

Figure 8.3 Three-mile pace table.

Newton's Three-Mile (5,000-Meter) Pace Table

3 mi	5K	1/4	1/2	3/4	mi	1 1/4	1 1/2	1 3/4	2 mi	2 1/4	2 1/2	2 3/4
20:40	21:25	1:42	3:26	5:10	6:53	8:37	10:23	12:08	13:53	15:34	17:16	18:58
20:50	21:35	1:43	3:28	5:12	6:56	8:41	10:28	12:14	14:00	15:41	17:24	19:07
21:00	21:46	1:44	3:29	5:15	7:00	8:45	10:33	12:20	14:07	15:49	17:33	19:16
21:10	21:56	1:44	3:31	5:17	7:03	8:50	10:38	12:26	14:13	15:56	17:41	19:25
21:20	22:06	1:45	3:33	5:20	7:06	8:54	10:43	12:31	14:20	16:04	17:49	19:35
21:30	22:17	1:46	3:34	5:22	7:10	8:58	10:48	12:37	14:27	16:11	17:58	19:44
21:40	22:27	1:47	3:36	5:25	7:13	9:02	10:53	12:43	14:33	16:19	18:06	19:53
21:50	22:37	1:48	3:38	5:27	7:16	9:06	10:58	12:49	14:40	16:26	18:14	20:02
22:00	22:48	1:49	3:39	5:30	7:20	9:10	11:03	12:55	14:47	16:34	18:23	20:11
22:10	22:58	1:49	3:41	5:32	7:23	9:15	11:08	13:01	14:53	16:41	18:31	20:20
22:20	23:08	1:50	3:43	5:35	7:26	9:19	11:13	13:06	15:00	16:49	18:39	20:30
22:30	23:19	1:51	3:44	5:37	7:30	9:23	11:18	13:12	15:07	16:56	18:48	20:39
22:40	23:29	1:52	3:46	5:40	7:33	9:27	11:23	13:18	15:13	17:04	18:56	20:48
22:50	23:39	1:53	3:48	5:42	7:36	9:31	11:28	13:24	15:20	17:11	19:04	20:57
23:00	23:50	1:54	3:49	5:45	7:40	9:35	11:33	13:30	15:27	17:19	19:13	21:06
23:10	24:00	1:54	3:51	5:47	7:43	9:40	11:38	13:36	15:33	17:26	19:21	21:15
23:20	24:10	1:55	3:53	5:50	7:46	9:44	11:43	13:41	15:40	17:34	19:29	21:25
23:30	24:21	1:56	3:54	5:52	7:50	9:48	11:48	13:47	15:47	17:41	19:38	21:34
23:40	24:31	1:57	3:56	5:55	7:53	9:52	11:53	13:53	15:53	17:49	19:46	21:43
23:50	24:41	1:58	3:58	5:57	7:56	9:56	11:58	13:59	16:00	17:56	19:54	21:52
24:00	24:52	1:59	3:59	6:00	8:00	10:00	12:03	14:05	16:07	18:04	20:03	22:01
24:10	25:02	1:59	4:01	6:02	8:03	10:05	12:08	14:11	16:13	18:11	20:11	22:10
24:20	25:12	2:00	4:03	6:05	8:06	10:09	12:13	14:16	16:20	18:19	20:19	22:20
24:30	25:23	2:01	4:04	6:07	8:10	10:13	12:18	14:23	16:27	18:27	20:28	22:30
24:40	25:33	2:02	4:06	6:10	8:13	10:17	12:23	14:28	16:33	18:34	20:36	22:38
24:50	25:44	2:03	4:08	6:12	8:16	10:21	12:28	14:34	16:40	18:41	20:44	22:50

Figure 8.3 *(continued)*

Chapter 9

DEVELOPING A RACE STRATEGY

Cross country is two events in one. It's an individual race awarding places and (for the leaders) prizes. But it's also a team race awarding points for runners' finishes. The two parts have somewhat different requirements. Chapter 8 dealt mainly with individuals and how they can run their own best pace. Now we talk about running together to minimize team points; this is a rare sport where fewer is better.

Cross country is unusual in another way. Other team sports put only two teams and 10 to 22 athletes on the court or field at one time. Here you might compete in a field of 25 or more teams and 200-plus runners at once. Because of this crowd, and because all of your runners are doing the same distance at the same time, team tactics come into play in cross country more than they do in track. Runners and coaches alike often say the team's high finish means more than the individual's, but you can't have one without the other.

DEVELOPING INDIVIDUAL TACTICS

My general tips to athletes about their tactics can be summarized this way:

1. Avoid starting too fast. Make a move through the field as the early pace begins to lag.
2. An exception to the advice above: When the race is run on a narrow trail where passing is difficult, establish position early. Sprint at the start if required.
3. Once you are out of sight around a corner or over a hill, increase the pace. Discourage followers who will see later that they have unexpectedly lost ground and give up the chase.
4. Pass opponents just before coming to a single-file area on the course. Don't let them slow down the pace here.
5. On windy days, run closely behind opponents. Let them break the wind.
6. When running behind other athletes, never watch their feet. Keep the head up and look at what's going on.
7. When opponents start carrying their arms higher during a race, assume they are tiring. Pass them then.
8. While passing, always give the impression of being fresh. Increase the pace slightly, and hold it until well ahead and unable to be repassed.
9. "Check out," which means increasing the pace for a few strides. Use this technique as a way to gain a physical and mental lift as well as to get the jump on an opponent.
10. Become a sprinter instead of a distance runner at the finish by making the necessary changes in running form. Finish as if the line were 10 yards past where it actually is.

DEVELOPING PACK RUNNING

Of the two aspects of cross country, team and individual, team is by far the more important.

That's my view and the guiding principle at our school. Cross country is the ultimate team sport. Sometimes I even hold our top runners back so the team runs together. This works to the detriment of the super athletes, but it also helps the slower ones to become overachievers as they work to keep up with the team's pack.

The team that trains together races together. We practice togetherness almost every day, with the athletes only running apart from the pack on Sundays. We warm up together, run intervals together, take our interrupted long runs together, do Saturday's segment workout together, cool down together. The top seven run as a group, and all the others stay within their groupings. Pack running becomes the rule for everyone on our team as soon as they arrive here and becomes second nature to these runners.

Our runners talk to their teammates during the races, encouraging each other. The captain sometimes even takes roll call at the mile: "Smith?" "Here." "Jones?" "Here." At other times they do lots of visual checking to see where everyone is.

Ideally the runners stay bunched together in meets. But practically speaking, it doesn't usually work out that perfectly. You don't want your fastest runners to sacrifice themselves by holding back in the state meet, for instance, where they might help the team more by placing in the top five individually. And you don't want everyone else to wait up for someone who is really lagging.

We don't expect everyone to cross the finish line side by side. But we do put a lot of emphasis on the time spread between the first and fifth scorers. I like to shoot for a 30-second difference, and it often works out this way.

DEVELOPING START TACTICS

At every meet most athletes go out like they have the devil nipping at their heels. They run the first stretch at an all-out sprint, hitting the first quarter under 60 seconds. That's sub-four-minute mile pace! It's hard for young

The men of York keep in a tight pack while preparing for a time trial in October 1996.

runners to keep their heads while others around them are losing theirs. But I tell our runners how counterproductive the sprint start is.

We obviously can't simulate mass starts in training, but we can and do work on steady pacing all the time. We put this into practice at all our meets. In addition, the runners constantly hear from me how well our way has worked in the past.

We're *never* out front in the beginning. In fact, at the state meet we often take a "one-thousand-one" count at the gun before starting to run. We do this if we drew a bad starting box and want to avoid traffic. We're dead last at the start, and people say, "Look at the York runners. They're out of it already." But we have won nine state championships after starting this way.

There are two other advantages of the "one-thousand-one" count besides staying out of traffic early on:

1. It eliminates the usual pattern of these meets: sprint start, jog for recovery, then a finishing sprint. We're able to pace the race steadily while picking off the fast starters as we go.
2. It allows our runners to stay with their teammates. Without the delayed start they could easily lose each other in the crowd and never see the runners they've trained and raced with all year. Running side by side with teammates gives them a sense of security in the race, where they need it most.

Starting Late

Knowles Dougherty once asked me to write about our "one-thousand-one" strategy for the *Cross Country Journal*. I reprint portions of that article here with his permission.

The women of York run in spite of the snow at the 1993 state meet at Detweiler Park.

In Illinois 27 large-school teams qualify for the state meet. These plus individual qualifiers result in a field of 229 athletes who are eligible to take the line each year. At the gun the runners go about 600 yards on a downhill straightaway. Then they make a 180-degree turn and come right back to where they started.

Here's the problem: The teams in the first 19 starting boxes must get outside of a chalk line or get trapped behind a snow fence early in the race. This means they must wait for everyone to go past or try to blast their way in among the crowd of runners who are punching and shoving. They can get hit, knocked down, or spiked.

For years I thought about how we could solve this problem. Our runners could go out with the crowd and hope for the best, or they could fight for the lead and risk going too fast. Year after year the front-

runners hit the 220 mark in about 23 seconds, which was too fast even for a downhill start. I didn't want our people starting that way.

So in 1977 we decided to try something different. It happened that we drew a bad starting box and had little chance of winning that year anyway. A radical experiment wouldn't cost us the title.

I said, "You know what we are going to do, men? We're taking a one-thousand-one count when the gun goes off, and we're letting everybody go out ahead of us. Then we're going to round the first curve free and easy. Even though we're dead last, we won't get cut down, we won't get our shoes knocked off, and we won't have to walk around the first curve. We'll be able to run our own race. Let's try it!"

Fortunately the runners accepted this plan. It worked out beautifully, and we ended up second in that state meet, even though we were seeded fifth or sixth. We've since won nine state championships while starting this way after drawing bad boxes.

DEVELOPING MIDRACE STRATEGY

Rarely does anyone pass a York runner during a race. We do the passing, and it's much more fun to pass than to be passed. It gives a sense of having momentum on your side. I tell our runners, "Don't pass unless you mean business. If you're going to pass someone, do it with authority and don't slow down as soon as you get by. Keep going at that pace!"

Your team is only as good as its fifth runner, the final scorer. At the state meet we set goals for where we want our top five to be at various checkpoints. We'd like to put all five in the top 50 after the first mile. By the two-mile point, we want them to be in the top 35; by 2 1/2 miles, all in the top 30; at the end, five in the top 25. When you pack five runners that far up, you're going to be hard to beat. I'm at each of those checkpoints myself. I tell the runners, "You look at me, and I'll let you know where you stand."

The homestretch is where fitness, racing savvy, and determination make themselves felt. Dozens of points can be gained or lost in the final quarter mile.

Kicking In

In 1986 we didn't have one runner make All-State, an honor given to the top 25 finishers. Our top runners, Scott Brooks and Kevin Buhrfiend, placed 26th and 27th. They just maintained their position in the homestretch and didn't let anyone outkick them.

But another of our scorers, Roger Peto, passed 50 runners in the last half mile, and 15 of them in the last 150 yards. He saved

our skin with his kick. We won another state championship by six points, and without Roger's heroics we probably would have finished no higher than third. It was one of the most fantastic finishes I've ever seen by a York athlete.

DEVELOPING RACE PLANS

How much focus you put on beating certain runners on certain teams depends on the meet. From the duals to the conference championships, you can assign each runner someone to try and beat on the other team.

We do this at the smaller meets. But it's impossible at State and some of the big invitationals. There it's a mass of humanity, and the runners might never even see the person they're supposed to beat. In this situation I just tell our athletes, "Run your own race. Stick to our plan."

Knowing your competition is important, of course. But it isn't practical, and maybe not even necessary, to send a scout to watch their meets. For one thing, we have raced against most of the teams in our area before we get to the season's big meets. So we already have a good idea how we match up against them.

We also check the meet results throughout the state. I absolutely want our runners to know who all the great runners and teams are throughout the state. We put on the bulletin board all the meet results we can get, and I talk about them at team meetings. We know how tough the courses are, what the times are worth, and who's hot and who's not. By the time we get to the state meet, we have a pretty good line on everyone we'll race against there. The opposition doesn't spring many surprises on us by this time.

DEVELOPING TEAM GOALS

You hope the runners agree with you that team success is more important than individual glory. The first thing you want them to

The women of York, 1995.

ask when they cross the finish line is, "How did the team do? Did we win?" And only after they've heard that answer should they ask, "What was my place? What was my time?"

Winning for All

We're consumed by the concept of team. It's the ultimate for us. The team trophy means so much more than an individual medal to me and, more importantly, to the athletes. Dave Walters was on our winning team as a sophomore in 1994. This was our sixth straight title, and it broke the state record for consecutive wins.

Dave was our cocaptain in 1996. I asked him at the start of that season, "What's it like to hold up that championship team trophy at the state meet?" He answered, "Pure, 100 percent ecstasy." He also made All-State as a junior and senior, and he said, "It doesn't mean a thing if the team doesn't win."

Part IV

COACHING FOR COMPETITIONS

Letter from a former York athlete to Joe Newton's team:

I wish you seven runners the same luck that our teams had at the state cross country championships. Since I've run in the race you are about to run, let me give you some advice:

1. Do not think you have to be a hero. You don't have to make a magical transformation into a runner you are not. Remember, this is a team sport, and if each person runs up to his ability you will all be heroes in the end.

2. Run your race. No other race of the year will have had as many runners, and no other race will have had as many stupid runners. Do not make the same foolish mistakes they do.

3. Have fun out there. In my best races I actually enjoyed the feeling of passing people and performing for the crowd. Find that thrill inside of yourself.

4. When the race is over, remember to thank each other and your coach. Together you have come a long way since you started running, and together you have made some of the sweetest memories of your lives.

Mark Olson

Class of 1995

Chapter 10

PREPARING FOR MEETS

Though training is vital, this chapter isn't about training. Though racing tactics are crucial, this isn't about racing. I've already discussed those essentials.

I talk here about something equally important: what happens after the heavy training is finished and before the actual racing begins. This chapter is about the mental and logistical preparation for competition. Though the tips offered here can be used at any meet, the emphasis is on the biggest meet of the season. In our case this is always the state championships, but at your school it could be the conference or another meet.

The preparation for typical meets is simpler because we're not traveling overnight and we're not tapering our training as much. But we still know who we're up against in *every* meet. We know what the course is like. We have a pacing plan for everyone.

For the biggest meets of the season the training tapers down the most, and the excitement builds the highest. Your role as a coach at this time is to bring the runners to a simultaneous physical and mental peak. In the final days and hours before The Big One, you use the train-down-and-psych-up routine that leads runners to the starting line. Then they make the final climb to the mountaintop.

PREPARING FOR PEAKING

Training is essentially finished with the state meet a week away. But the workouts taken will still have value as confidence-builders.

We reduce the volume of training by about 50 percent in that last week. I've toyed with the idea of reducing it even more but haven't had the nerve to do that just yet. Our mileage drops, along with the number of intervals. The last hard workout is on Monday, when we do a mile time trial, rest 10 minutes, then run another mile at good speed.

"You've done a similar workout four Mondays in a row," I tell our runners. "Look how much your times have improved in that period." I add, "This should be your easiest race of the year. You're the best prepared for it and the most rested for it."

Stan Reddel, the sprinting coach for the York track team, is always eager to help the cross country team during home meets.

PREPARING FOR THE BIG ONE

Here's our last workout of the year as a full team, the Thursday afternoon before the state meet:

- Jog five miles
- Calisthenics
- Six × 100 meters
- Three × 400 meters (62, 60, 56 seconds) with three-minute interval
- 300 meters
- 20 × 100 meters
- Jog two miles single file, with chant

These are my team-meeting notes for that last day at home before the state meet:

1. Wear suit and tie going down to Peoria.
2. Run four miles tomorrow morning.
3. Turn in sweats today.
4. State meet runners bring luggage to school.
5. Report to gym at 10:55 A.M. for 11:15 departure.
6. Go back to P.E. class on Monday.
7. Begin winter conditioning on Monday.
8. Introduce seniors on their last night and tell them: "Each line you cross tonight is another obstacle you have overcome in life. Each curve you run is another corner turned in your life. It is not an empty field out there. Ghosts of all who have gone before are behind each tree. Now you will join them. I will do anything for you, always."

PREPARING BY PSYCHING

You want to work on the runners' minds this whole week. We use a number of tactics to accomplish that goal.

I bring in guests. The most prominent of these is Peter Coe, Olympic gold medalist Sebastian's father and coach, who has come to visit the team four times in the final week. Our guests usually come on the last day of

Loosening up before a 1996 race.

practice, which is a Thursday. We have a very light workout, but it's a day dripping with emotion and tradition.

One of the traditions is that *everyone* on the team continues to practice, even though the season has ended for most of these runners. They give support to the runners going to the state meet. In our final cool-down all 135 athletes run single file and give a team chant that we've developed. This sends chills up everyone's spine.

Then we give out our team awards for the year. This is handled by the captains, and anyone is eligible to win one of about 100 prizes. The program eases the worries about the state meet, because we're all having so much fun.

Honoring Others

Our kids dedicate their state meet race to someone who has had misfortune. They decide who it will be and announce it on the final night of practice. When we win, that person gets a gold medal.

One year they chose a young man from a neighboring school, Michael Pesola,

who'd suffered a stroke. He came to the state meet in a wheelchair that fall and vowed he would walk the next year. And he did.

Another kid, Brian Wagner, was a football player at York who came out for track as a junior. That summer he was killed in a car wreck. I told his mother, "If we win the state championship, we're going to give the trophy to you in honor of Brian." We did, and she was extremely moved by the gesture.

On Friday morning we leave for State. Several classes are let out, and we have 100 to 200 people yelling for the runners as they climb into the vans to start our trip. By then we're very well aware that we are running for many more people than ourselves.

You also have to psych runners *down* somewhat if they start to grow too anxious. High school kids make mountains out of molehills, getting so nervous that they risk psyching themselves out. We want them to be aggressive and have some nervous tension but don't want them to fall apart mentally.

Freshmen Donald Sage and Mike Lucchesi running in tandem in the 1996 Aurora sectional.

A big plus for us is that we run at the Peoria Invitational on the state meet course one month before the big meet. I say to the runners in the last week, "You've had another four weeks of training and can run a faster time. But you don't have to go faster. Just do the same and we will be in the hunt."

I'm constantly emphasizing that they don't have to get all panic-stricken. They don't need to hammer the heck out of the course or try to exceed themselves. No big breakthrough is required. They only have to run up to the potential that they showed a month before. I tell them, "Just be yourself—no more, no less."

PREPARING TO TRAVEL

It sometimes seems like we're planning a military campaign. We have the whole thing down to a science, both because it eliminates possible glitches and because it puts the runners' minds at ease to know they don't have to think about any of this. Their coach takes care of all the logistics. I arrange for vans through car dealers in town, phone the hotel and restaurants, plan the menus, and arrange the schedule down to the minute.

Our traveling party numbers 32. We take the seven competitors plus eight underclass alternates (who race among themselves Friday on the state course) and four managers. The others are adults. They include a policeman who works at York. He goes along to ensure that no problems arise during the weekend.

We arrive at the meet site about two o'clock in the afternoon, check into the hotel, dress for running, and go right to the course. The alternates run their race while the State team has a light workout. They warm up with three miles on the actual course and the usual six × 100 meters. Then they run six × 200 from the starting line, matching the opening pace that we want them to run the next day. We know by Friday what our starting box will be, so we run some of the 200s from that box.

The trick for keeping nervous runners in check at the hotel is to allow them very little down time. Don't give them a lot of idle hours to sit and brood. When we come back from the workout, they shower, change into their suits, and go out to dinner. After that they attend a movie together. The only time I'm not with them is when they go out for ice cream after the movie, then return to the hotel for their own team meeting. Once they're back in their rooms, I stop at each room and talk to each pair of roommates for a few minutes.

PREPARING TO RACE

What you do on race morning will depend on when the race starts. Our state meet isn't run until 12:45 P.M., so we don't need to get up too early. We go out for a little 15-minute run, then come back and get ready for breakfast. After eating, we take a 15-minute walk to stretch out the legs and shake down the meal.

John Janulis finishes at a Downers Grove North dual meet at York's East End Park.

A little later the runners suit up in their meet uniforms and come to my room for a team meeting. Here we go over the race plan one last time. Again you try to de-emphasize the result. You focus instead on the plan: Here's what the runners are capable of doing, here's where we expect them to be when. I constantly tell them: "Be yourself today. Don't try to exceed your limits."

A favorite story of mine has to do with the leaves on a tree. Look at the tree in early October and it's filled with leaves. By late October, half the leaves are gone. Then in November only a few leaves remain. "I want you to be like those last leaves," I'll tell our runners. "I want you to be hanging on to the very end, refusing to fall off the pace."

The minute-by-minute planning really comes into play during the prerace warm-up. We leave for the course an hour and a half before the race, which gives us time to walk out from the finish and note the distance checkpoints that we've measured: a quarter mile to go, 150, and so on.

Our warm-up always starts exactly 35 minutes prior to the race. It begins with a two-mile jog. Calisthenics start with 17 minutes to go. Then, at 13 minutes out, we do our six 100-meter surges.

Eleven minutes left: Now we change into our spikes and meet shirt at the team bench, a picnic table about 300 meters from the finish line. Alumni runners come by the bench and wish our athletes well. Our fans, 1,000 to 1,500 of them, crowd around. The band plays our school song, the cheerleaders cheer. It's an awesome scene.

With six minutes to go, they jog to the starting line. I meet them there with four minutes to go. They line up in their starting box, four in front and three in back. I shake hands with each runner.

Then I tell them all, "Remember your race plan. Stay with your teammates. We'll count your points later." They take two short runouts from the starting line. Two minutes to go now, and I say, "See you later."

Newton's State Meet Itinerary

Friday, November 8, 1996

11:00 a.m.	Meeting in York Gym
11:15 a.m.	Leave York High School
2:15 p.m.	Arrive Peoria and check in at Red Roof Inn
2:45 p.m.	Out to Detweiller Park to loosen up
4:15 p.m.	Back to motel and shower
5:15 p.m.	Eat dinner as a team at Old Country Buffet
6:15 p.m. - 9:00 p.m.	Go to a single feature movie
9:15 p.m. -10:00 p.m.	In rooms
10:15 p.m.	In bed

Saturday, November 4, 1996

7:15 a.m.	Team arises
7:30 a.m.	Across the street and run 15 minutes around the parking lot
7:45 a.m. - 8:15 a.m.	Shower and dress
8:30 a.m.	Breakfast as a team at Doc's Mt. Hawley Inn
9:15 a.m. - 9:45 a.m.	Split into groups and walk
9:45 a.m. -10:15 a.m.	Back to motel and rest and dress
10:15 a.m. -10:30 a.m.	Team meeting in Mr. Newton's room
10:45 a.m.	Leave for Detweiller Park
11:00 a.m.	Arrive at Detweiller Park
11:00 a.m. -11:45 a.m.	Walk the course
12:10 p.m. -12:35 p.m.	Warm up
12:40 p.m.	Report to starting line
12:45 p.m.	RACE BEGINS...LET'S GO YORK!!
9:00 p.m.	Arrive home

REMEMBER ONE THING . . .

WE ARE NOT GOING TO PEORIA TO HAVE A BALL!!!!!!!!!!!
WE ARE GOING TO PEORIA TO WIN OUR 20TH STATE CHAMPIONSHIP.

TO DO THIS, WE MUST HAVE A GREAT TEAM EFFORT WITH TOTAL CONCENTRATION ON RUNNING UP TO OUR POTENTIAL. THE TEAM THAT GOES IN WITH A REAL DESIRE TO WIN IT, AN ATTITUDE OF MENTAL TOUGHNESS ABOUT WHAT THEY CAN DO, AN AGGRESSIVE APPROACH TO THE RACE, AND A WILLINGNESS TO RUN WITH THEIR ABILITY AND CHALLENGE THE OTHER TEAMS WILL WIN. TO PARAPHRASE SEBASTIAN COE, "WE ARE FROM YORK OF ELMHURST AND NO BLOODY B------S ARE GOING TO TAKE THE STATE TITLE AWAY FROM US."

REMEMBER, SCIENTISTS SAID THE BEE COULDN'T FLY BECAUSE ITS WING SPAN WAS TOO SHORT, BUT THE BEE DIDN'T LISTEN—IT FLEW. PEOPLE WHO BELIEVE (LIKE THE BEE) ARE INVINCIBLE!!!!!! LET'S BE GREAT!!!!!! NOW IT'S *YOUR TURN* TO ADD TO THE STRING. WE ARE A TEAM OF *DESTINY* OUT TO MAKE HISTORY . . . BY RETURNING THE STATE TITLE TO ITS RIGHTFUL HOME. . .

YORK HIGH SCHOOL

Newton's Handy Alibi Sheet

Runners need to take their sport seriously but also need to take a little time to laugh at themselves. With this in mind I hand them this alibi sheet that provides almost any explanation they might need for a subpar performance. The idea, of course, is never to have to use any of the alibis.

_____ ate too much
_____ weak from lack of nourishment
_____ not enough time to warm up
_____ warmed up too much
_____ not enough training
_____ overtrained
_____ not enough sleep
_____ too much sleep
_____ needed wheat germ oil
_____ needed yogurt
_____ needed vitamin C
_____ not enough weight training
_____ too much weight training
_____ building up slowly for next year
_____ don't want to improve too soon
_____ saving myself for (name of event)
_____ bus too crowded; couldn't relax
_____ car too crowded; got leg cramp
_____ bus too quiet
_____ started kick too soon
_____ started kick too late
_____ couldn't kick
_____ worried about girl
_____ worried about money
_____ worried about studies
_____ girlfriend unfriendly
_____ girlfriend too friendly
_____ saw (name) was running and choked
_____ I didn't think
_____ I thought too much
_____ (name) cut me off
_____ I cut him off and thought I was DQed
_____ I fell down
_____ I'm a mudder and it was too dry
_____ can't run in the mud
_____ they all jumped the gun but me
_____ thought they would recall us at start
_____ poor starter
_____ poor finish judge
_____ poor course
_____ footing too soft
_____ footing too hard
_____ too warm
_____ too cold
_____ shin splints
_____ blisters
_____ sore knee
_____ sore back
_____ headache
_____ forgot my shoes

_____ snow-blinded
_____ cold feet
_____ thought I had a heart attack
_____ fogged glasses
_____ thought I had another lap to go
_____ ran an extra lap
_____ can't run when behind
_____ can't run when ahead
_____ can't run
_____ too much competition
_____ too many meets
_____ not enough meets
_____ no medals awarded
_____ medals too cheap to work for
_____ too many people depended on me
_____ no one cared how I did
_____ don't like organized athletics
_____ only run for exercise
_____ only run for fun
_____ didn't feel like running
_____ felt great, and that's a bad sign
_____ couldn't get excited about race
_____ I was overanxious
_____ my mind was too tense
_____ my mind was too relaxed
_____ my coach doesn't understand me
_____ I don't understand my coach
_____ I don't like my teammates
_____ my teammates don't like me
_____ looking forward to indoor track
_____ looking forward to outdoor track
_____ looking forward to next year
_____ I slipped at the start
_____ I can't stand too much success
_____ I can't stand failure
_____ I have emotional problems
_____ I never had to run so hard before
_____ had a bad cold
_____ can't run longer than 200 meters
_____ had to stay home to babysit
_____ can't keep up the pace
_____ don't know pace
_____ I thought I had desire
_____ guess I don't have the courage
_____ drank too much pop yesterday
_____ not enough salt in my system
_____ I have to quit to get a job
_____ have to quit to get better grades
_____ my doctor told me not to run
_____ my mother told me not to run

Chapter 11

COACHING MEETS

Once the race begins, you slip into the role of spectator. You're a highly interested and involved fan, to be sure, but not too different from other fans on the course that day. You can't call time-out during a cross country race to discuss strategy. You can't send in a substitute to relay your message to the team.

Once the race starts, your runners are pretty much on their own. It's their race to run as best they can. You only get to stand beside the course at select points, updating their progress and shouting encouragement. Now you must trust that you've prepared your athletes well and that they will carry out the race plan you've worked out together. When you next talk to them, at the finish line, it will be too late to change anything that happened this day.

COACHING ON THE COURSE

As your runners go to the starting line, you can expect to be as excited, and as nervous, as they are. They have a race plan, and so must you.

Another great thing about cross country is that the coaches and spectators don't stay in one place, but follow the action. You see people running all over the course on raceday. My plan is to stay with our runners as long as possible before the race. I don't want to just turn them loose in these final minutes when they need me there.

We separate shortly before the gun goes off. Then I'll watch them pass various points along the course. We try to rendezvous at least two or three times, which I believe to be very important. This means I really have to scramble to get to these various spots.

It was fairly easy to get around when I still ran every day, but now with my bum knee a

The York women's team camps out.

fast walk is my best pace. Even then I'm sweating like the devil, and my heart is pounding about 200 beats a minute as the race goes on. It's really thrilling.

At most meets the last time I see our runners is at about 2 1/2 miles. You can't see the finish line from there and can't know for sure how the team did. But I have a pretty good idea from where they stood and how they looked with a half mile to go.

COACHING DUTIES

You can do very little actual coaching during the race itself. Look at it this way: The race lasts 15 minutes or more, and the coach makes contact with the runners for maybe 15 *seconds* of that time.

We're prohibited from calling splits at our state meet. But I can tell the runners whether they're on pace or off pace. And I can tell them their place, how many people they need to pass, and roughly where we stand teamwise. The kids look for me, see me, hear me, and I yell something to each of them.

Of course, the routine differs if you're in charge of conducting the race. Coaches put on their race-director hat when meets are run at home. These duties might keep them from doing any coaching out on the course that day. But I've been very lucky this way. Gary Goss, who ran for York in the mid-1960s, now conducts all of our home meets, from lining up volunteers to doing the scoring. Gary has a foolproof system worked out, and he leaves me with nothing to do except coach.

One of the most neglected arts is that of staging a cross country meet. How many times in your experience have you run in a meet with no chute or a chute that is highly inadequate? How many times have you run in a meet where officials got the placings, scoring, or timing mixed up? How many times have you run in a meet where only first place was timed? How many times have you run in a meet where no results were announced?

I could go on and on with this list of failings, but I've made my point: Conducting a cross country meet involves much more than just showing up at the course. We as cross country coaches have a product to sell, just as any salesman does. What better way to sell cross country than by making your meets a real spectacle for runners and fans alike? I'm a firm believer that every cross country meet can be made into a thrilling event if you present it properly. Here I present ideas on proper meet organization.

Start with a checklist of all equipment needed for conducting a meet (see figure 11.1). This ranges from ropes and poles for the finish chute, to cones and flags for the course, to watches and score sheets for the results. Collect this gear well in advance of race time. Also set up the course well ahead of time, giving special attention to marking the route clearly and erecting an adequate finish chute (see figure 11.2).

Line up a crew of officials for raceday. At York we typically use the following: one starter, two timers, one time checker, three scorers, one recorder of results, one announcer. For big meets we add one extra scorer, three judges on the course, two people to hold ropes at the mouth of the chute in case of jam-ups, six people to push runners through the chute, and three custodians of awards. I realize that it can be hard to line up help for meets. But we owe it to ourselves, to our runners, and to our sport to get the job done right.

When we have a meet at York, we bring out the cheerleaders and band, and as many spectators as possible. We also erect a banner welcoming the visiting teams. We assign a student to each team in the meet. This host gives them their scoring tags and pins, shows them the course, and answers questions. The host is their guide throughout the meet.

Our announcing starts 15 minutes before race time. We give time checks at 15, 10, 5, and 2 minutes. This helps the runners in their warm-up. Before the race the starter explains the course and answers any questions the runners might have. The starter also alerts them to what splits will be called.

At the finish we make absolutely sure that everyone's time and place are recorded accurately. This is done with a simple but effective scoring system that we've used for more than 30 years. In this system each runner is given a tag to pin on the front of his shirt. The tag includes name and school, with space to write the finish position (see figure 11.3).

Officials in the chute pull these tags as the runners finish. Then they are numbered in order of finish and clipped on a scoreboard for tabulation of team scores (see figures 11.4 and 11.5). Meanwhile the timers read the times to the runners as they cross the finish line. These are recorded by place and later added to the scoreboard (see figure 11.6).

We insist on announcing results and presenting team and individual awards right away so the crowd will still be there. This makes the runners feel important and gives them the recognition they deserve.

So there you have it: a properly set up course, plenty of meet officials, a band playing, cheerleaders and fans cheering, welcoming banners and team guides, and fast scoring. This is how cross country can and should be presented.

COACHING COMMENTS

You want to be positive while still being honest in what you say to your runners as they pass you on the course. Occasionally I'll yell at runners, "Move up! You're killing us!" because they're not racing up to their potential.

But in general I'll shout things like, "You're looking great!" or "This is your day!" They'll tell me later, "I couldn't hear a thing on the course except your voice." My wife calls it my "coach's voice."

There are also certain things you *avoid* saying. For instance, you don't demean the other teams. I'm sensitive to this because it has happened too often to us. "Beat that York dork!" someone will shout. I try never to say anything like that. The most I'll do is point out, "You have two runners from such-and-such school right in front of you. Catch them!"

Cross Country Meet Checklist

When conducting a meet at our school, we make sure that the following equipment and supplies are on hand.

☐ Posts for constructing the finish chute.

☐ Sledge hammer for setting the posts.

☐ Towels for padding the first two chute posts.

☐ Ropes for the chute area.

☐ Extra ropes to extend the chutes, if necessary.

☐ Rope to enclose the scoring area.

☐ Red cones for marking the course.

☐ Flags for additional course marking.

☐ Limer to mark the course.

☐ Scoreboard for scoring the meet.

☐ Scoring tags and paper clips.

☐ Score sheets.

☐ Three clipboards.

☐ Three stopwatches.

☐ Chronomix timing device (if you have one; if not, then time sheets for recording results).

☐ Starting gun and shells.

☐ Microphone or megaphone to announce results.

☐ Victory stand for awards at big meets.

☐ Course maps for visiting teams.

☐ Large banner welcoming visiting teams to the course.

Figure 11.1 Meet checklist.

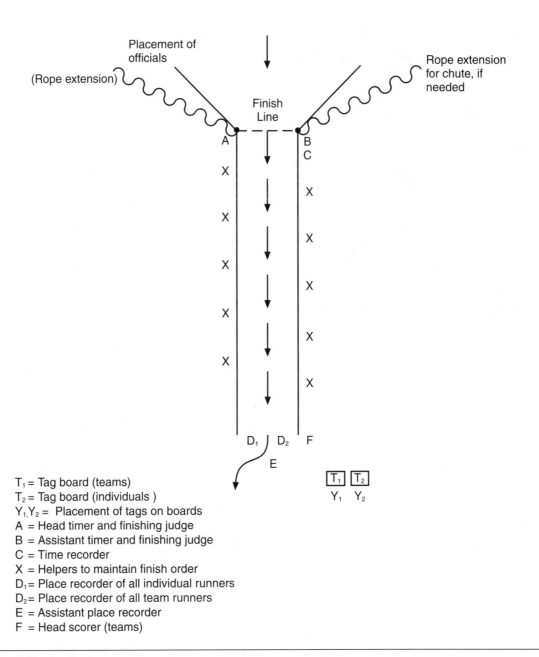

Placement of
officials

(Rope extension)

Rope extension
for chute, if
needed

Finish
Line

A   B
C

X

X   X

X   X

X   X

X   X

X

D₁ D₂   F

E

T_1 = Tag board (teams)
T_2 = Tag board (individuals)
Y_1,Y_2 = Placement of tags on boards
A = Head timer and finishing judge
B = Assistant timer and finishing judge
C = Time recorder
X = Helpers to maintain finish order
D_1= Place recorder of all individual runners
D_2= Place recorder of all team runners
E = Assistant place recorder
F = Head scorer (teams)

Figure 11.2 The finish chute.

COACHING AFTERMATH

Let's take the state meet as an example of what the coach does after the race. The last time I see our runners is with a half mile to go, and then I'm in suspense as to the outcome.

The runners pass through the chute and get a card with their place on it. Then they meet me back at the team bench and hand over the cards. We start figuring the score but don't make any judgment on it. I speak to the runners for a few minutes, give them a hug, and congratulate them if they ran well or try to pick them up if they ran poorly. Then they go off for their cool-down as we await the results.

We don't let them skip the cool-down, even when it's the last and biggest meet of the season. They jog two miles. At the state meet they're usually a mile or so out when we get word of the score. If we won, the band breaks into the school song. Then we'll see the runners jumping up and down, rolling on the

Figure 11.3 Dean Foote wears a team tag and Chuck Weigel wears an individual tag.

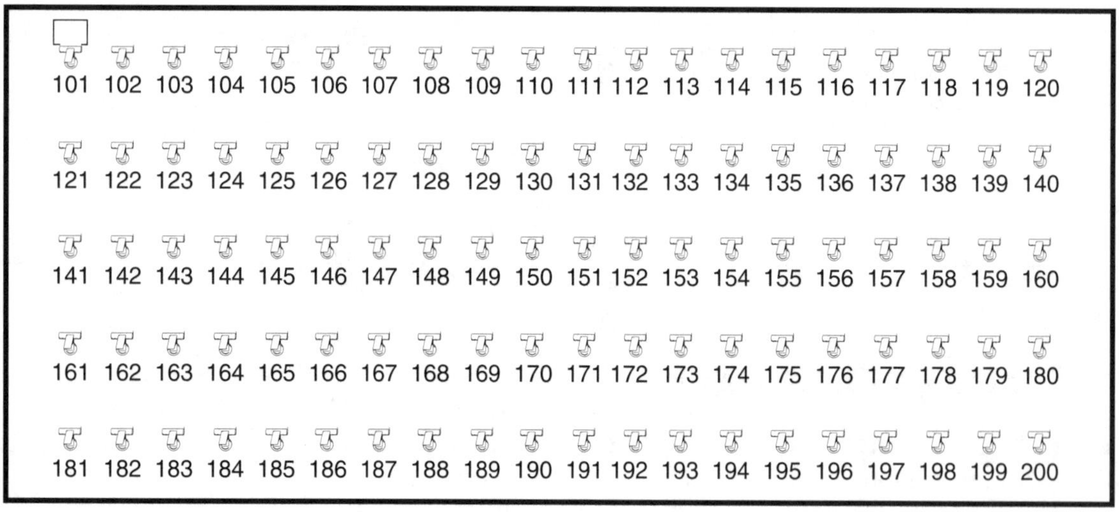

Figure 11.4 Team board for places 101 to 200.

Individuals – order of finish (only)

1	2	3	4	5	6	7	8	9	10
11	12	13	14	15	16	17	18	19	20
21	22	23	24	25	26	27	28	29	30
31	32	33	34	35	36	37	38	39	40
41	42	43	44	45	46	47	48	49	50

Figure 11.5 Individual tag board. Note: First place tag is in place.

Team scores   **York District C.C. Meet**   Date:

Team A	Team B	Team C	Team D	Team E	Team F	Team G

Team H	Team I	Team J	Team K	Team L	Team M	Team N

Figure 11.6 Scoreboard that the scorer hangs around his or her neck.

Chris Gorski, Al Kabat, Brian Vercruysse represent the York pack in the 1989 state meet.

ground, and sprinting back toward the team area at a pace faster than some of them had finished the race.

You don't need to wait for the official results. You can do some pretty accurate scoring yourself.

Knowing the Score

Michael Newman, an All-State runner for us in 1979, comes back to help at the finish of all our meets. He goes right down to the chute area and does his own scoring, which is invariably accurate. I don't believe anyone else until Michael gives us the word. This usually takes him about 15 minutes at the state meet, which is much quicker than the officials with their computers can do it.

Then if we've won, the band strikes up, the runners come sprinting to the team area, the fans gather around, and the celebrating begins. Limos pull up, win or lose, and the athletes go back to dress in their tuxes if we've placed in the top three teams.

The race doesn't end at the finish line. You should expect as much class from your runners after the event as they displayed during it. If we win, we're humble in victory. If we lose, we're gracious in defeat.

We always attend the awards ceremony at the state meet, even if we don't win a trophy for a top-three finish. And we always make a point of congratulating the winning team, even though very few teams ever congratulate us

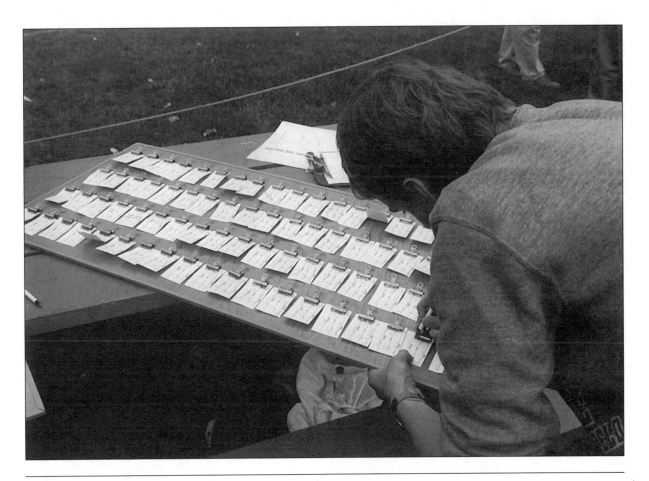

All scores must be carefully added.

when we win. No public sulking is allowed if we lose and no gloating if we win.

Newton's State Meet

Team Meeting

Every year we have a team meeting in my hotel room approximately 2-1/2 hours before we run the state cross country meet. These are notes from our 1996 meeting.

1. Read jobs and review pace charts.
2. As soon as we get there, we will measure 110, 150, 220, 300, 440, and 600 yards to go.
3. We will warm up at 12:10 P.M. Run a controlled warm-up. Run 110s hard.
4. Discuss race plans. Go out fairly fast and gradually move to the right. After the first turn move up gradually over next 600 yards. We must run together all the way.
5. Concentrate on the means (race plan), and the results will come. Races are won in the middle if you are in position to take advantage of it. This is where we break the race wide open.
6. With 229 runners the meet is not as crowded as the Peoria Invitational. Many will choke, but our athletes won't be among them.
7. Remind them, "You're tough, and you are ready. The secret is running up to your potential, nothing more, nothing less. Just be yourself and do not panic."
8. York has a great tradition of super state meets. We have done it 19 times. Our

goal is three All-Staters and 85 points, 5 in the top 30.

9. "Remember, no one passes you from 600 yards on in."

10. Run the last 440 yards with reckless abandon. Don't look back. Go into chute tough.

11. Play the game with 300 to go. Every runner passed means "win."

12. Give a second effort in the sprint. Raise the knees and let the jaw hang loose.

13. Size and speed do not win races. Heart and desire get it done.

14. Who are those people who win? Those who when their lungs are bursting keep going. They are like leaves in the fall. One always hangs on to the very end.

15. No bells, no whistles, no smoke, no mirrors. Just being the best is good enough. Don't let mental weakness overcome physical strength.

16. After the race go right to the team area and turn in place cards. Sweats on and jog a mile while waiting for results.

Part V

COACHING EVALUATION

Letter from a former York athlete to Joe Newton:

Running has been part of my life for the last 10 years. But I have always run by myself. Failure in races, success in races—it didn't really concern anyone but me. Through this year at York, my attitude has changed dramatically. At the end of the track season my only concern was to win the state meet as a team.

After 10 years of individual competition you made me a team player. It is unbelievable what can happen when a team is backing you and cheering you on. If I ever become an Olympian, you will be the person who got me there. You made me realize what I can do. I will now work with determination toward my dreams and goals, thanks to you.

Please keep coaching as long as you can. You are a true example of how much one person can do if he dedicates himself to a task. Yours is coaching, and your achievements have been incredible.

Marius Bakken

Class of 1996

(In 1996 Marius Bakken, an exchange student from Norway, became the first runner in the 102-year history of the Illinois State Track Meet to medal in all three distance races—winning the 1,600 and 3,200 titles while placing second in the 800. He had placed fourth in the state cross country meet the previous fall.)

Chapter 12

EVALUATING RUNNERS' PERFORMANCES

One beauty of running as a sport is that it doesn't keep you guessing. An accurate time for a measured distance leaves no doubt about the relative value of performances. Coach and athlete have many ways to judge times. They can compare each runner against others on the team, against other teams, and against the history of all runners who ever competed at this distance or on the same course.

Mainly, though, runners compare themselves with their own standards. How fast did they run this year versus last? How much did they improve during this season? A runner who improves, wins. The greater the progress, the bigger the victory. In this chapter we talk about how to maximize, measure, and reward individual improvement. Chapter 13 deals with team progress.

EVALUATING IMPROVEMENT

Evaluating starts with keeping individual records for *every* runner on the team. The two greatest letters in this sport are *PR*. They of course stand for *personal record*, and that allows everyone to succeed by improving. I talk all the time about PRs. It's my favorite phrase.

"You might never score a point for the team, never win a medal or a ribbon, never get your name in the paper," I tell our runners. "But every time you set a PR, you're a winner."

We announce PRs every day. This especially gives the little people the feedback they need. It lets them feel good about themselves because they know they're making progress. Keeping track of PRs means maintaining voluminous records. I keep three sets of books: a brown book for workouts, a red one for race times of each individual, and a blue one for team results. I'm an old-fashioned coach who does this all by hand with pen and paper instead of on a computer. It takes lots of time, but it is time well spent.

EVALUATING "WINNING"

My definition of "winning" is simple. Runners win by doing the best they can with the ability they have. In every race only one person wins by crossing the finish line first. But that doesn't mean everybody else is a loser. Everyone who runs can win on their own terms.

EVALUATING PROGRESS

The first day of team practice at York I ask all the runners to list their goals for the season. Most of them who have been in the program are realistic about what they can accomplish. Some, however, err in one direction or the other, either by setting goals too high or too low. Only then do I step in and suggest revisions.

How much progress do you expect runners to make from year to year? The biggest jump comes between the freshman and sophomore year. That's when the cumulative effects of a

Even though he was not part of the top seven, James Sheridan's spirit for the team made him the 1995 captain.

year's training make themselves felt, and when kids tend to mature quickly. They're also familiar with the program and with the demands of racing by now.

Typical improvement from the freshman to sophomore year is one minute in the two-mile and two minutes for three miles. I like to see about a 30-second drop in three-mile times from sophomore to junior, then another 30 seconds as a senior. Some people improve more than that. Then there are others who mature early and level off after their sophomore year.

What is normal progress from the first to final race of a season? You want the runners to have a sense of building momentum during the season. Ideally each race will be faster than the one before, with the last one being the fastest. This is one reason why we go into our early-season races a little tired, so the athletes can't run too fast too soon. We take a chance of losing meets by doing it this way. We hope for a 45-second drop in three-mile times during the season. Most of our runners hit that target as they freshen up and peak at the end of the year.

Improvement isn't guaranteed, however. Some of the best freshmen don't stay in the program. One of the fascinations and frustrations of coaching is that you never know how a runner will grow.

Improving Dramatically

Cases of dramatic progress bring joy to a coach's heart. They make all our work worthwhile. As I write, we have a runner named Dominic Bruno. He came in weighing 180 or 190 pounds, and one year later he was down around 140. In that year he brought his two-mile time down from 13:32 to 11:19. Dominic will never be one of our top runners. But I'd like to have 80 or 90 guys who get the most from their ability like him.

Another athlete I recall fondly was Dan Ruecking, who's now at the Naval Academy. As a freshman Dan was one of our bottom 10 runners, but as a senior he was number one on our team and finished in the top 10 at State. He's a living example that by being persistent and having good work habits, you can climb to the top of the mountain.

In every cross country meet, splits are recorded for the top runners.

EVALUATING AWARDS

Of the many postseason awards we give based on performance, two are the most prized. These are "Most Valuable Runner" and "Most Improved Runner."

Most Valuable Runner doesn't necessarily go to the top runner on the team. Instead we give it to the person who gets the job done in every meet. He's The Rock of the team, the one you can always count on. Most Improved Runner goes to someone like Dominic Bruno, an overachiever who exceeded everyone's expectations but his own. The fifth runner on the sophomore team is just as likely to win it as an All-Stater.

As for awarding letters, different schools have different philosophies on this. We happen to think that anyone who puts in the effort deserves a letter, an honor with value that everyone in school recognizes. Our standard for a letter is scoring five points. Runners earn a point by beating the fifth runner from the other team in a dual meet. In a big meet they get one point just by running and finishing. Placing in the middle third of the field there is worth two points; the upper third, three points.

We also award junior varsity letters and freshman numerals. I do everything in my power to see that as many runners as possible earn letters.

EVALUATING GOALS

Future goals take two forms. One is for the underclassmen and what they plan to do next year. The other is for graduating seniors who want to continue their running careers.

We don't have any formal meetings with either group. They just come into my office one by one, when or if they wish. Hardly anyone comes in for the first couple of weeks. They want to get away from the sport then. After that they start trickling in. We talk about what the returnees can do to get better and where they might fit into the team's goals the next fall.

Moving On

For those seniors who have the talent and desire to run in college, I field the calls and letters from coaches and pass it along to the runners. If they seek counseling, I'll give it. If the athlete is interested in a particular school that hasn't contacted him, I'll call the coach. It's part of my job to spend this time working on the runner's behalf.

They've done everything I asked in training and on the racecourse. Now it's my turn to do anything for them—*forever*, and not just up to the point where they stop scoring points for the team.

One of our all-time top runners, Marius Bakken, came as an exchange student from Norway and didn't know anything about the U.S. college system. I hooked him up with Sam Bell, one of my heroes, at Indiana University. Marius went down on a recruiting trip, fell in love with the place and with Sam, and is now going to Indiana.

EVALUATING EXCELLENCE

The following ingredients of excellence were taught to me by Peter Coe, who coached his son Sebastian, a two-time Olympic gold medalist at 1,500 meters:

1. Great champions and great teams acquire a reputation and an aura of invincibility. Remember, when the very best step onto the starting line, the rest know they are competing for minor places.

1996 York pack at the first dual meet of the season. Leading are Phil Olson, Pat Jordan, Mike Marinier, and Noah Lawrence.

2. Do not be arrogant, but have total self-confidence. The best will not yield to the rest.

3. Pursuit of being number one is a hard road to follow. Mental conditioning must include learning to be pressure-proof.

4. If a runner is going to compete with a driving but controlled aggression, it must rest on hard-won strength. This cannot be obtained from wishing, only from hard work.

5. Practice leads to perfection. The racing whole must be broken down into separate parts, with each one practiced and honed to a fine edge.

6. Each athlete is an individual. Pick out individual weaknesses and work to eliminate them, giving priority to those elements that will yield the greatest improvement in performance.

7. Don't train to train; train to *race*. Do the same in workouts as in races: run hard.

8. Run fast at the end of a race when tired. Always sprint at the end of any distance workout.

9. Championship running calls for sustained high speed. Since speed is the name of the game, never get too far away from it in training.

10. When doing road runs and fartlek, never let the pace slacken. Would-be champions cannot afford too many slow road miles.

11. Run fast in practice. Long slow distance (LSD) creates long slow runners.

12. The most specific training for fast running *is* fast running. It doesn't matter if runners can run 200 meters in 21, 22, or 23 seconds; can they do it at the end of a race?

13. Pick one workout considered an acid test of readiness for major competition. Ours

is eight $\times$ 300 meters in 40 to 43 seconds with a one-minute interval.

14. Distance running is endurance based, but runners also need speed and strength. Squats are a must for distance running.

15. In regard to injury: when in doubt, *don't*.

16. Do not run too many races. Only race when it will enhance development.

17. Overracing will take a runner to the line underprepared. The more important the race, the higher the peaking and the longer the preparation period and tapering-off time.

18. All races call for tactics. Smart tactics depend on runners knowing what is happening all around them.

19. There is a tendency to slow down in the third quarter of a race. Learning to keep going all-out when the body is screaming to stop is essential to becoming a champion.

20. Races vary a lot with changes in pace and effort; there are sudden demands for anaerobic power well above normal. Training must equip a runner to meet these peak demands.

21. Races unfold rapidly. Good decisions are made by runners who stay alert and maintain concentration.

22. Have patience and come along slowly. Runners are like wine; if they don't spoil when young, they will get better with age.

23 The mental aspect of running is very important. Always run to win.

24. Really great and consistent winners are those whose only satisfaction comes from success. Winning isn't everything, but wanting to do one's best is.

Chapter 13

EVALUATING YOUR PROGRAM

A runner's race doesn't end at the finish, but with a cool-down. Likewise, a coach's season doesn't end with the last meet, but in the cooling-out period afterward. That's when you review the season. The sooner you do this, the clearer the appraisal. What went right, and what went wrong? Which practices do you want to continue next year, and which need enhancing or dropping?

Frankly, when you're as successful as we have been over the years, you don't make many big changes. I'm from the old school that believes, "When it ain't broke, don't fix it." But the program still requires regular fine-tuning. For instance, one year we unexpectedly fell apart at the state meet. In hindsight I saw that the runners needed more practice on pace and more mental training to believe they were state-championship material.

No sooner does one season end than preparation begins for the next one. Many of the athletes have run their last cross country race for you and must be replaced. Much as you become attached to the runners, they come and go all too quickly. You stay, and the program goes on.

EVALUATING "SUCCESS"

What "success" is for you depends on your program's history and expectations. It could be winning *one* meet, having a winning dual-meet record for the season, winning the conference, or qualifying for the state meet.

Our goals are really lofty because we've done so well in the past. We want to win the state meet every year. In fact, we're *expected* to win it; anything less is a failure in some people's eyes. This is the monster we've created for ourselves. I'm not complaining about high expectations, though. We have the same high goals. You have to set them high or you never get off the ground.

The only way a team can "fail" is if it doesn't live up to its potential. This happens when a team beats *itself*. I can live with getting beat at the state meet. I don't like it, but I can accept it if the runners compete up to their potential and finish behind a better team. But if we let down and beat ourselves, then I'm very, very disappointed. It has not been a successful season.

EVALUATING THE SEASON

No matter how the season has gone, I feel relieved when it is over. That's normal. Just as the runners are tired from a long season and look forward to a break, so does the coach. For the last two months of the racing season I've been all fired up. In another two months I'll be fired up again for indoor track. But right now I need to get away from the daily training and the weekly meets for awhile. The coach needs to regenerate as the runners do.

The problem comes when a couple of months have passed and you still aren't excited about starting another season. *That's* abnormal. If you want the kids to be enthusiastic when they come back for another season, you'd better work on rediscovering your enthusiasm. If you can't find it, perhaps you're in the wrong line of work. Shortly after Christmas break I'm chomping at the bit, ready to see what indoor track holds for us.

The time between seasons, when we're not spending three hours at practice each afternoon and weekends at meets, isn't really free then. It's just used differently. The coach's job goes on, and this time is devoted to other parts of it. This is my busiest time in the office. The Monday after the season ends, I'm right back in the office for those three hours in the afternoon. If you rest while other coaches are working, you put yourself at a disadvantage.

My major project in that interim period is the postseason book. I spend at least six

The York women after earning a perfect score of 15 at the Fenton Regional.

weeks compiling it, hoping to have the book ready to distribute to our athletes by early January. I spend lots of time evaluating the season while compiling this book containing all the results from this year and records from past years. The kids also use it to evaluate their own running and to study their competition. It gives them motivation to start training hard again for track (see figures 13.1-13.2).

EVALUATING THE RETURNEES

The off-season is a good time to talk with returning athletes about what will be expected of them next year, because they aren't caught up in the heat of battle then. Some of them need help to get over physical problems, some are feeling a little jaded mentally, and some just want to come by and talk. I listen to them more now than I did as a young coach. They give great feedback on what the team is thinking, especially by telling me what's going on in their private lives that might be affecting their performances.

Awaiting Their Time

At York a runner doesn't have a very long moment in the sun. We're a senior-dominated team, and most kids only have one year to really shine. I tell those who'll be seniors next year, "Now it's your turn."

For instance, I had a kid named Bob Reed who wasn't much of a runner early in high school. No one from any other team knew who he was. Then as a senior in 1990 he caught fire and led us to the state title.

Remember the movie *Butch Cassidy and the Sundance Kid,* where they kept asking about their pursuers, "Who *are* those guys?" That's how it is with our team. People who never heard of these runners wonder where they came from, not realizing that we spent two or three years nurturing them for this moment in the sun.

A coach always has to look ahead, because as soon as one season ends, you've lost part of that cross country team to graduation. You already must start thinking about rebuilding for next year. A month after our season ends, I have the next season plotted out. I've looked at every team we'll race—who it lost and who's back. Our kids do the same.

You can't rest on your laurels, or you're going to lose. You always have to plan ahead. If the season hasn't gone as well as you'd hoped, you indulge in second-guessing yourself. A season never goes perfectly, so there's always room for you to improve.

I make mistakes and try to admit them and correct them. But at this stage in my career it's rarely necessary to make revolutionary changes in the program; small adjustments will usually be enough. This old dog is still capable of learning new tricks. I still pick up ideas from other coaches at clinics and from reading books and magazines. After four decades of coaching, I'm still looking for the winning edge.

EVALUATING YOUR FUTURE

No coach is irreplaceable. The best you can hope to do is leave the program in better shape for your successor than it was when you took the job.

As I said in the first chapter, my goal is to coach until the year 2000. That will stretch my career over six decades and two centuries. By then I'll be in my 70s and ready to pass the torch to a new coach. Two years later the kids won't know who Joe Newton is. Young runners live in the present and near future, not in the past—which is as it should be.

"The Long Green Line"
1994 IHSA State X Country Champs

York of Elmhurst

**West Suburban Conference, Fenton Regional,
Aurora Sectional, Illinois State Champions**

6 Straight- "We Fixed On Six"

Figure 13.1 1994 postseason book cover.

Summary of the 1994 York High School Cross Country Season

MEMORABLE MOMENTS
1. YORK'S WINNING THE 1994 ILLINOIS STATE MEET FOR THE 19TH TIME.
2. YORK'S WINNING THE 17TH STRAIGHT WEST SUBURBAN CONFERENCE CHAMPIONSHIP.
3. YORK'S WINNING 3 LEVELS IN THE WEST SUBURBAN CONFERENCE MEET.
4. YORK'S WINNING THE PALATINE INVITATIONAL FOR THE 2ND YEAR IN A ROW.
5. YORK'S WINNING THE PEORIA INVITATIONAL FOR THE 19TH TIME.
6. YORK'S WINNING THE FENTON REGIONAL AND THE AURORA SECTIONAL TITLES.
7. BRIAN GARY AND SRINU HANUMADASS MAKING ALL-STATE.

"FIX ON SIX" AND "DO IT FOR DAN" WERE OUR WATCHWORDS FOR 1994 . . . AND YOU DID IT!!! IT WAS A SPECTACULAR ENDING TO A VERY TRYING YEAR. YOU FACED MUCH ADVERSITY ALONG THE WAY AND YET YOU MET EVERY CHALLENGE. YOU CERTAINLY PROVED THE OLD ADAGE THAT "ADVERSITY MAKES THE MAN." WORDS CANNOT ADEQUATELY EXPRESS THE FEELING WE ALL HAD AS WE CELEBRATED ATOP THE PICNIC TABLE . . . WITH OUR FANS CHEERING WILDLY AND OUR BAND PLAYING THE "SAINTS" SONG. WHAT A VERY SPECIAL MOMENT IN TIME.

OUR CHAMPIONSHIP WAS MORE MEANINGFUL BECAUSE IT ALLOWED US TO PRESENT THE CHAMPIONSHIP TROPHY TO DAN CASEY IN MEMORY OF HIS WIFE ROSE . . . A VERY TENDER MOMENT THAT GAVE HAPPINESS IN HIS TIME OF NEED. THE LAST 3 WEEKS OF THE SEASON, WHEN WE "CIRCLED THE WAGON" (HAMBONE'S QUOTE) YOU LEARNED A VERY IMPORTANT FACT . . . THAT GREAT TEAMWORK IS THE ONLY WAY TO REACH OUR ULTIMATE MOMENTS, TO CREATE BREAKTHROUGHS THAT FILL YOUR LIVES WITH A SENSE OF LASTING SIGNIFICANCE.

I WANT YOU TO REMEMBER THAT WE SET A NEW STATE RECORD BY WINNING OUR 6TH STRAIGHT STATE CHAMPIONSHIP. YOU HAD A MISSION THAT WE ALL BELIEVED IN AND IT FUELED YOUR MOTIVATION AND INSPIRED YOU TO ACT . . . BECAUSE OF YOUR ENDURANCE, YOUR FOCUS, AND YOUR HARD WORK YOU NOW HAVE THE PRIVILEGE OF KNOWING THAT WHAT YOU DID REALLY COUNTED, REALLY MATTERED. YOU UPPED THE ANTE TO AN UNBEATABLE EXCELLENCE THAT GAVE US A CHAMPIONSHIP TEAM. . . . YOU HAVE NOW BECOME HISTORICALLY SIGNIFICANT AND HAVE LEFT FOOTPRINTS FOR ALL TO FOLLOW.

IT HAS BEEN MY HONOR TO BE YOUR COACH. I WILL ALWAYS HAVE A PLACE IN MY HEART FOR "BALTZIE," "ALEX," "FASAN," "FOLKIE," "BRIAN G.," "BIG HAL," "HAMBONE," "OLIE," "RILES," "RUSS," "SCHULTZIE," "SWAINER," "JO-JO," "VAL," "MATT M," AND "EDDIE." AMONG THESE NAMES ARE SEVERAL WARRIORS WHO WERE WILLING TO SACRIFICE SUPERFICIAL SELF-INTEREST IN ORDER TO UNDERWRITE THE BUILDING OF A TEAM THAT SUPPORTED YOUR SKILLS.

THE GIFT CERTIFICATE, TAPES, AND MOTOR SEAT CUSHION THAT CAME FROM THIS 1994 TEAM WERE JUST SUPER. I THANK EACH AND EVERY ONE OF YOU.

LET US NEVER FORGET THE 7 BOYS WHO HELPED US WIN THE 1994 STATE CHAMPIONSHIP: BRIAN GARY, SRINU HANUMADASS, DAN JORDAN, PHIL RUSSO, DAVE WALTERS, DAVID MARINIER, AND MARK OLSON . . . THESE ARE THE NAMES THAT WILL ALWAYS BE IN THE YORK HALL OF FAME. THEY WILL FOREVER SERVE AS AN INSPIRATION TO EVERY YORK CROSS COUNTRY RUNNER TO WEAR THE GREEN AND WHITE.

IT IS WITH A GREAT AMOUNT OF PLEASURE THAT I DEDICATE THIS BOOKLET TO THE 8 BOYS WHO WENT FAR BEYOND THE CALL OF DUTY BY RUNNING 1,000 MILES THIS SUMMER . . . AND FINALLY TO OUR GRADUATING SENIORS, WE WISH YOU SUCCESS AND HAPPINESS IN ALL YOUR FUTURE ENDEAVORS.

Joseph Newton

Joseph Newton
Head Cross Country Coach

Figure 13.2 1994 postseason letter.

INDEX

ABOUT THE AUTHOR

Joe **Newton** is without question the most successful high school cross country coach in the United States. He started his scholastic coaching career in 1954 in Waterman, Illinois, before moving on three years later to York High School in Elmhurst, Illinois, where he's been ever since. In his 42 years at York, Newton has built a running dynasty. His boys' cross country teams have won an unprecedented 18 national championships, 19 state championships, and 113 conference titles. They have also won an impressive 98 percent of their home meets.

Newton's coaching accomplishments have earned him a long list of awards and honors. He was named National High School Cross Country Coach of the Year by the National High School Coaches Association in 1975 and by the National Federation of High School Administrators in 1994. In addition, he has been named High School Cross Country Coach of the Year 16 times by the Northern Illinois Track Coaches Association and 15 times by the Illinois High School Coaches Association. In 1988, Newton was chosen as one of the coaches of the U.S. men's track and field Olympic team in Seoul, South Korea. He was the first high school coach to ever receive this honor.

Known as a master motivator, Newton is a frequent guest speaker at corporate meetings and social gatherings around the United States. He has delivered his message of teamwork, commitment, and discipline more than 5,000 times. He has also put his philosophy of coaching and life into print in his three books: *Running to the Top of the Mountain, The Long Green Line,* and *Motivation: The Name of the Game.*

Coach Newton lives in Naperville, Illinois, with his wife Joan. When he's not winning cross country meets, he enjoys reading, working out, and touring the Old West.

Joe Henderson has been writing about running for more than 30 years. He's not only the West Coast editor and a featured columnist for *Runner's World* magazine but also the author of more than a dozen books on running, including *Better Runs*, *Long-Run Solution*, *Fitness Running,* and *Jog, Run, Race*. In addition, he writes and produces a monthly newsletter called *Running Commentary* and is an adjunct assistant professor of journalism at the University of Oregon. Henderson lives in Eugene, Oregon.

LEARN HOW TO BE A COMPLETE COACH

with these books from the American Sport Education Program

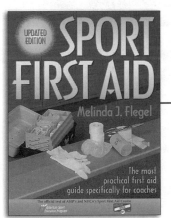

ISBN 0-88011-556-4 • 200 pages • 1997

Contains the latest guidelines and procedures that coaches need to become competent first responders to nearly 100 athletic injuries.

ISBN 0-87322-715-8 • 208 pages • 1996

Explains to coaches how to set a positive example, establish and enforce an effective athlete code of conduct, use their position as coach to involve others in drug prevention efforts, and respond effectively when an athlete needs help.

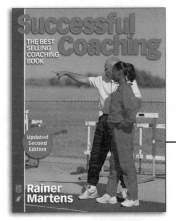

ISBN 0-88011-666-8 • 232 pages • 1997

Contains information on developing a positive coaching philosophy, applying the principles of sport psychology and sport physiology to coaching, teaching sport skills properly, and using management skills effectively.

ISBN 0-88011-512-2 • 128 pages • 1997

Provides coaches with a valuable tool to help them understand the basic principles of sportsmanship, the justification of these principles, and how to teach their players to understand and apply them.

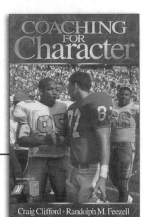

American Sport Education Program

Guides to Better Running

1997 • Paperback • 208 pp
Item PGRE0406
ISBN 0-87322-406-X
$18.95 ($27.95 Canadian)

Filled with more than 100 helpful tables, illustrations, and photos. Helps coaches and runners understand how much to run at various stages of development and how to design appropriate training programs.

TRAINING FOR YOUNG DISTANCE RUNNERS

TECHNIQUE · CONDITIONING · RACING

Foreword by Joe Newton

LARRY GREENE & RUSS PATE

SECOND EDITION

Better Training for Distance Runners

Forewords by Sebastian Coe and Anne Marie Lauck

David E. Martin, PhD · Peter N. Coe

1997 • Paperback • 464 pp
Item PMAR0530 • **ISBN 0-88011-530-0**
$22.95 ($33.95 Canadian)

Provides a prescription for success for today's competitive distance runners and their coaches. Combines cutting edge research, sound training principles, and proven program strategies to improve performance in events ranging from the 800-meters to the marathon.

1996 • Paperback • 264 pp
Item PHEN0866
ISBN 0-87322-866-9
$15.95 ($22.95 Canadian)

Practical suggestions on every aspect of running—from how to choose the right shoes to how to set up an effective training program. Time-tested advice and amusing anecdotes to guide and motivate.

BETTER RUNS

25 YEARS' WORTH OF LESSONS FOR RUNNING FASTER AND FARTHER

FOREWORD BY JEFF GALLOWAY

JOE HENDERSON

Human Kinetics
The Premier Publisher for Sports & Fitness
http://www.humankinetics.com/

Prices subject to change.

To request more information or to place your order, U.S. customers call **TOLL-FREE 1-800-747-4457**. Customers outside the U.S. use appropriate telephone number/address shown in the front of this book.